The Apollo Moon Missions

Hiding a Hoax in Plain Sight

Part I

First Edition
Copyright © 2018 by Randy Walsh
ISBN#9781790584444

No part of this publication may be reproduced, broadcast, transmitted, distributed or displayed; except for brief quotations in reviews without prior written permission

Note: The author has made every effort to make sure that the quotations from literary and artistic works of other authors made in this work are within limits of fair practice as defined by Article 10 of the Berne Convention for the protection of Literary and Artistic Work.

All quotes and pictures used to the extent allowed by fair use. Should any copyright issues arise, or you just want to make a comment, please contact the author, Randy Walsh at:

✉ authorrandy@hotmail.com

f @authorrandywalsh

Cover Page: The images have been cropped and edited digitally to fit the book layout. Credit – NASA & Wikipedia/Wikimedia

Back Cover Photo: "Courtesy Photo & Framing", by Mr. J.P. Kendhari {T#1-416-398-3955}

Table Of Contents

Introduction	7
Chapter 1 - Apollo 11: An Overview of The Official Story	**14**
The Apollo 11 Astronauts	15
The Launch	18
Lunar Orbit and Landing	19
Lunar Liftoff	20
Back to Earth and Splashdown	21
Chapter 2 - The Saturn V Rocket	**24**
The Apollo Saturn V Program	28
History	29
Wernher von Braun And His Alleged War Crimes	30
The Apollo Saturn Rocket Series Starts With Tragedy	32
The Overrated Power Of The Saturn V F-1 Engines	40
Minimal Testing Of The F-1 Engines	41
Former Rocketdyne Employee Bill Kaysing Exposes The F-1 Fraud	47

Engineer Gennady Ivchenkov Ph.D.,
Substantiates Bill Kaysing's Claims   50

Alexander Popov Ph.D. And Andrei Bulatov
Prove the F-1 Fraud With Apollo 11 Film   58

S. G. Pokrovsky, Ph.D. Comes To Similar
Conclusions With The Official Apollo 11 Film
Footage   61

The Minimal Testing Of The Saturn V   63

Summary   67

Chapter 3 - Navigation And The Apollo Guidance Computer   73

Fly-By-Wire   74

Apollo Guidance Computer   76
    1. The Inertial Measurement Unit   77
    2. The Optics   78
    3. Guidance, Navigation And Control System   80

Trajectory And Docking Using the
Non-Autonomous AGC   81

The Astronauts Would Have Been
Marooned In Cislunar Space   82

Tracking Apollo Missions, The NASA Way   85

Theatrics At Its Best   87

Charts And Slide Rules   89

The Limited Capacity And Memory Of The AGC   90

Where Exactly Is The Equigravisphere?   94

Redundancy - Hand And Eye Coordination   96

Summary   97

Chapter 4 - Radiation Belts Around The Earth, Intense Solar Storms & Galactic Cosmic Rays
                                                                  101

Basic Theory   101
    The Rad And The Rem   106

Van Allen Radiation Belts   107
    Discovery Of The Van Allen Belts   108
    Conflicting Information Regarding
    Intensity Of The Van Allen Belts   109
    Outer Electron Belts Would Have
    Exceeded Apollo Spacecraft Shielding   117
    Clash Of The Titans   119
    Three, Maybe Four, Radiation Belts   125

                                                                  130

Solar Particle Events
    SPE Basics   131
    Maximum SPE Activity During Apollo Missions   132
    SPEs Are Unpredictable   136
    More Conflicting Information   137

Coronal Mass Ejections   140

Galactic Cosmic Rays   141

A Quote Here, A Quote There   144

Summary   150

Chapter 5 - Shielding For Radiation, Thermal Control, And Micrometeoroids   154

Command And Service Module Dimensions And Shielding   158

Lunar Module Dimensions And Shielding   160

Temperature In Space   163

The Apollo Spacecraft Environment And Thermal Control   165
    Atmosphere Revitalization System   166
    Thermal Control System   167
    NASA Contradicts Itself, Yet Again   170
    PTC Would Not Have Worked   171

NASA Reveals It Knew Little About The Space Environment	172
Micrometeoroid Shielding	173
The Pegasus Missions	174
Moving The Goal Posts	175
Summary	176
Chapter 6 - Conclusion	181
Missing And/Or Destroyed Documents	181
The Missing Or Destroyed Saturn V Documents	184
Missing Apollo 11 Telemetry Tapes	185
Telemetry From The Moon	186
Missing, Destroyed, Or Never Existed, Take Your Pick	189
The Soviets (Russians) To The Rescue, Well Maybe	194
In Conclusion	194
Glossary	200
Bibliography	202

Introduction

Like a lot of people my age, I remember sitting in school with the anticipation of what was probably the most significant scientific achievement in history, or at least, the 20th century. It was the morning of July 16, 1969 and we were waiting to be led to join another class to watch the launch of Apollo 11 on, what I remember to be, a grainy black and white TV. I was in awe, not fully understanding what was being shown but still having some understanding of the importance of it from what our teachers told us.

From that point on, I became interested in space and as I was already an aviation enthusiast, I began adding model spaceships to my collection of model airplanes.

For decades, I was enthralled by aviation and manned space missions and always tried to stay informed. However, as with most people, my interest in space technology waned by the time I was in my 30s, preoccupied with daily routines and just trying to pay the bills.

By the late 1990s, I didn't really give space missions all that much thought until one evening, when I turned on the TV and noticed a documentary on one of the Apollo Moon missions being aired. I'm not clear on the details, given that this documentary aired two decades ago, but one thing in particular caught my attention. The Apollo astronauts being interviewed for this documentary talked about making sure they had the grid pattern on the window of the Command Module (CM) or Lunar Module (LM) properly lined up with the Earth. I believe too that they mentioned the slingshot maneuver around the Moon, which (more appropriately) is also called a gravity assist. This meant that they were talking about Apollo 13, since they had a serious situation involving the Service Module and they needed to use the gravity of the Moon to assist in a trajectory back to Earth.

One of the Apollo 13 astronauts in the documentary recounted about having made it clear to his colleague that when he fired the engine, he was to keep the Earth within the grid pattern on the window, no matter what. So, no doubt, they were using visual references. Considering the vast distance in cislunar space (the area of space between the Earth and the Moon's orbit), using visual references in conjunction with the newly designed fly-by-wire computer, was a precarious way of navigating, which surely would have led to disaster. I remember thinking that they should have had a little more sophistication in their navigational technique, considering the accuracy needed for such a vast distance.

By the time this documentary was shown, I had long given up model airplanes and spaceships for the real thing with my private pilot's license already in hand and with a commercial pilot's license on the way. Naturally I knew quite a lot about navigation techniques. I also knew how easy it was to move off track, left wondering where you were in no time. I realized that having an instrument rating, that allows a pilot to fly on instruments including the use of radio navigation, was more preferable and more accurate than using visual references on long cross-country flights. Now imagine using a newly designed computer that was supposed to have had state of the art technology, used on a mission 240,000 miles from Earth, by far the longest navigation track ever for any manned mission, while trying to keep Earth within a grid pattern on the window pane and dealing with a potential catastrophic situation with the spacecraft. Not exactly a precise way of obtaining and maintaining course. Not to mention the real possibility of being marooned in space for eternity using this technique. Even with the newly designed fly-by-wire computer system for navigation, visual references seemed to have been a necessary component, which for me, was the first indication that this computer used in the Apollo missions was not all that it was being made out to be.

From this point on, I had a renewed interest in the manned space program, especially the Apollo Moon missions. Eventually, I started reading the official narrative in books, as well as the 'conspiracy theory books', along with numerous articles and published reports, in an effort to get as much perspectives on these missions as possible. I started to notice inconsistencies, contradictory and conflicting statements from those directly and indirectly involved with the Apollo missions. Further, there was even more conflicting information from scientists and technical writers on the space environment and the technology used. After all, if NASA is going to risk the lives of astronauts in Low Earth Orbit (LEO) and beyond, that is, away from the protection of the Earth's magnetic field, one would expect scientists to agree on the data regarding such a dangerous and unpredictable environment, but as it turned out, they didn't.

There are numerous books written on the official narrative of these missions that provide many details, which is where a lot of the answers are if you want to get at the truth of what I now know was a hoax. Some of the books in support of the hypothesis that the Apollo missions were faked, get into the Freemasonry, numerology and conspiracy aspects of these missions, and they do it quite effectively. However, this book will not get into any of these aspects. Instead, this book is about the scientific and technical methods claimed to have been used in the Apollo missions and when taking a closer look at the details in those methods, we see how impossible it would have been:

1. To send manned missions beyond LEO and through the Van Allen Radiation belts

2. Being bombarded by Galactic Cosmic Rays (GCRs), Solar Particle Events (SPEs) and Coronal Mass Ejections (CMEs) and
3. Encountering micrometeoroids and thermal loads that pose a constant hazard to any manned mission.

After years of reading and studying the contradictory and conflicting information in the available material, as well as applying my skills as a Commercial Pilot and Flight Instructor, I concluded that the Apollo missions were faked. A lot of people with qualifications and expertise in other areas have come to similar conclusions. However, as I discovered, that information isn't as readily available in the established educational institutions or the mainstream media. But, it is there and elsewhere if you are prepared to look for it yourselves.

In **Chapter 1,** I present an overview of the official narrative and basic details of the Apollo 11 mission. However, I believe all the Apollo missions were faked, at least beyond LEO. I use the Apollo 11 mission, for the most part, as a template to discuss and question the technology and other aspects of the Apollo missions in sequence of how they supposedly happened.

Chapter 2 is about the heavy lift Saturn V rocket that was used in the Apollo Moon missions. I start off with a listing of the successes of the Soviet space program and a comparison to the American space program. I then discuss a brief but disturbing history of the scientists involved in the design and building of the Saturn V rocket, needed for a successful manned landing on the Moon. Also included, is the work of four scientists' analyses of the Saturn V rocket with its F-1 engines and their conclusions that this rocket did not have the power of sending a fully loaded Saturn V rocket to LEO, let alone, beyond. Further, I look into the questionable testing practices of the

Saturn V in the actual conditions of spaceflight before using it on a manned mission.

This chapter alone proves the hoax, but a comprehensive look at all of the aspects of the Apollo missions, which this book looks at in great detail, is a necessary response to the proponents of these missions.

Chapter 3 goes into detail about the Apollo Guidance Computer (AGC). I detail the navigation component of the AGC and the impossible tasks it was expected to perform in order to have safely navigated a manned mission to the Moon and back. As you'll learn in this chapter, the AGC did not have the necessary autonomous capabilities for such a manned mission.

Chapter 4 on the other hand discusses details about the Van Allen belts, Galactic Cosmic Rays (GCRs), Solar Particle Events (SPEs) and Coronal Mass Ejections (CMEs) as well as the contradictions and conflicting information from scientists inside and outside of NASA, regarding the intensity of the radiation in these regions of space. In addition, I point out the attenuation of radiation to acceptable levels for the astronauts, as was claimed by NASA. This attenuation of radiation was based on incomplete data regarding the Van Allen belts and other sources of intense radiation in cislunar space.

Chapter 5 continues with an analysis of the actual shielding of the Apollo spacecraft versus what shielding would have been needed to attenuate radiation to acceptable levels. I explain the basic theory regarding the temperature variation in the vacuum of space and the thermal control aspects of the Apollo spacecraft. From there, we dive into the details of the threat posed by micrometeoroids and see how, as with radiation, the CM and LM lacked the necessary shielding needed for the protection of the safety of the missions, and of course the astronauts. In this chapter you'll learn just how flimsy the LM was, so much so, that it's been reported that it wouldn't have been able to support its own weight here on Earth. At the end of this chapter it should become obvious that any one of the elements in the space environment, let alone encountering them all at once, would have meant disaster for any of the Apollo missions.

In **Chapter 6** we highlight the incomplete, missing and/or destroyed documents related to all of the Apollo missions.

Chapters 2, 3, and 4 start off with history, theory, technical details, and a description of the technology used. Some readers may find this a bit tedious, but I encourage you to persevere as I then go on to analyze the details that prove how impossible this technology would have been for the success of an Apollo manned mission to the Moon and back. I have minimized any conversions of measurements, unless they are used in quotes.

Part 1 of this series affirms that all of the Apollo manned missions outside of LEO were impossible, and therefore faked. That doesn't mean manned missions outside of LEO will never be possible since new technologies are being designed and developed all the time. But by inference, this book does raise some serious questions as to why these technologies for manned missions outside of LEO are taking so long to be developed, considering the successes that NASA claims to have had with sending nine manned missions beyond LEO to circumnavigate the Moon five decades ago.

It is claimed that when writing about subjects such as the Apollo Moon missions' hoax, that authors give the impression that they have inside information. I can assure you that I make no such claim. All the information in this book is out in the public domain: either in books, articles, videos, or any of the numerous sources of online information, including NASA's website. I have essentially condensed the numerous evident inconsistencies published by scientists and other professionals directly or indirectly related to the Apollo missions into a coherent text, while applying my own analysis.

I hope reading this book will encourage you to do further research on the subject. For most of you, I have no doubt that you will come to the same conclusion about the Apollo Moon missions as I have and that is, NASA has been **'Hiding a Hoax in Plain Sight.'**

Chapter One

Apollo 11

An Overview Of The Official Version

"Lights, camera, action!"

Between 1968 and 1972, the National Aeronautics and Space Administration (NASA) launched 11 manned missions on the Saturn IB & Saturn V rocket to low Earth orbit (LEO). Nine of these manned missions went beyond LEO using the Saturn V rocket and six landed on the lunar surface; Apollo 11 being the first mission to do so. The Saturn V was a three-staged rocket that stood 363 feet tall on the Launch pad. Each stage of the rocket had a specific function:

1. The first stage was filled with kerosene and liquid oxygen and had 7,653,845 pounds of thrust and was used to launch the Saturn V rocket to an altitude of 36.7 miles.
2. The second stage was filled with liquid hydrogen and liquid oxygen and had 1,120,216 to 1,157,707 pounds of thrust. After the separation of the first stage, the second stage was used to boost the Apollo spacecraft to an altitude of 101.4 miles.
3. The third stage was filled with liquid hydrogen and liquid oxygen and had 178,161 to 203,779 pounds of thrust. After the separation of the second stage, the third stage was used to insert the Apollo spacecraft into a circular Earth parking orbit. The Lunar Module (LM) was stored in the Spacecraft Lunar Module Adapter

(SLA) located on top of the third stage, the S-IVB. Above the S-IVB was the Command and Service Module (CSM).

The Launch Escape System (LES) was fixed to a Boost Protective Cover (BPC). The BPC covered the Command Module (CM) to protect it from heat friction with the air during the first three minutes of the launch and from the solid-fuel rocket motor of the LES. In the case of an emergency, the LES was used to pull the CM away from the Saturn V to safety, for an emergency splashdown.

A more in-depth look at the testing and performance aspects of the Saturn V will be discussed in Chapter 2.

Figure 1.1 – Launch of Apollo 11 (July 16, 1969)
Source: NASA

The Apollo 11 Astronauts

Apollo 11 was NASA's fifth manned mission in the Apollo program and the third manned mission which left LEO on its mission to the Moon. It was also the first mission to land a crew on the lunar surface. The crew included Commander Neil Armstrong, Command Module Pilot Michael Collins, and Lunar Module Pilot Edwin (Buzz) E. Aldrin. For each of the Apollo missions, there was always a backup crew. For Apollo 11, the backup crew consisted of Commander James A. Lovell, Command Module Pilot Williams A. Anders, and Lunar Module Pilot Fred W. Haise.

Neil Armstrong started flying at the age of 14, paying about 10 dollars for each lesson which lasted about 1 ½ hours. This today amounts to approximately 10 dollars or more for every five minutes! He got his pilot's license at 16. In 1947 he was accepted for a Navy scholarship and went to Purdue University in Indiana. After 18 months, the Navy sent him to Pensacola in Florida for flight training. In 1950, he flew combat missions in the Korean War. After the Korean war, he continued on for further flight training. In 1952, he resigned from the Navy and enrolled again at Purdue University. In 1960, Armstrong flew the X-15, which could reach altitudes over 200,000 feet, which he described as akin to being in a spaceship in orbit. After applying to NASA in 1962 in which the organization was now accepting civilian applicants, he was accepted for astronaut training.

Edwin Eugene Aldrin Jr., aka Buzz Aldrin, (his elder sister, when young, used to pronounce 'brother' as 'buzzer,' hence the name), went to the Military Academy at West Point, New York. After graduating in 1951, Aldrin joined the Air Force and trained as a fighter pilot. He also flew combat missions in North Korea. His gun camera film supposedly showed a pilot ejecting from a MiG he shot down, which was featured in Life

Magazine. In 1954, after spending four months in Maxwell Field, Alabama in squadron officer school, he was assigned to the Air Force Academy in Colorado as a flight instructor. In 1956, he went to West Germany to fly the F-100 with the 36th Fighter Wing. After that he returned to the USA and gained a postgraduate degree at the Massachusetts Institute of Technology in which he did a doctorate in astronautics. In 1963 Aldrin was accepted by NASA for astronaut training.

Michael Collins went to West Point, Louisiana. After graduating in 1952, he joined the Air force and was sent to Nellis Air Force Base in Nevada for fighter training. From there he was stationed in France at a NATO F-86 fighter squadron in 1954. After returning to the USA in 1957, Collins was assigned as an instructor. In 1960 Collins enrolled at the Experimental Test Pilot School, Edwards Air Force Base. He was accepted by NASA in 1963 for astronaut training.

Figure 1.2 – Apollo 11 Crew - Neil Armstrong, Michael Collins and Buzz Aldrin (L to R)
Source: NASA

Armstrong, Collins and Aldrin had been in the Gemini space program and two of the backup crew members, Lovell and Anders, also had previous experience in space most noticeably as crew members on Apollo 8, the first manned mission to have left LEO to circumnavigate the Moon. The responsibilities of a backup crew included taking the place of any astronaut who is unable to participate in the mission.

The Launch

The launch of Apollo 11 took place at 9:32 am EDT, July 16, 1969 from NASA's Kennedy Space Center launch Complex 39-A for an eight-day mission to the Moon and back. After liftoff, the first stage of the Saturn V was jettisoned at about 40 miles in altitude. The second stage was then ignited to boost Apollo 11 to a 100-mile orbital altitude. After reaching the required altitude and the jettison of its first and second stages, the first engine burn or firing of the third stage (S-IVB) would insert Apollo 11 into a 100 nautical mile circular Earth parking orbit. After 2 ½ hours in Earth orbit, the S-IVB's rocket would be fired again, putting Apollo 11 on a translunar insertion (TLI) for a free return trajectory for a three-day voyage to the Moon. Theoretically, the purpose of a free return trajectory was to insure a return to Earth in the event of a Service Module engine failure.

A half hour after TLI, the Command/Service Module (CSM) would separate from the S-IVB, turn around, and dock with the Lunar Module (LM) to extract it from the Spacecraft LM Adapter (SLA). After docking procedures, the CSM docked with the LM and would have resumed its course towards the Moon for its planned lunar orbit. At this point, Apollo 11 would be put into the Passive Thermal Control (PTC) mode. This was a slow roll of the spacecraft on its horizontal axis, thus stabilizing the thermal response to solar heating. This will be discussed in detail in chapter 5.

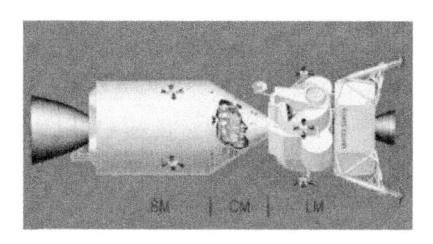

Figure 1.3 – Apollo 11 Command Service Module and Lunar Module
Source: Wikimedia

After reaching the Moon, Apollo 11 would then have been inserted into a 60 by 170 nautical mile elliptical orbit. Two revolutions later, the orbit would have been adjusted to a near circular orbit of 54 by 66 nautical miles. Both of these lunar orbit insertion burns (LOI) would have been made using the CSM's 20,500-pound thrust engine.

Lunar Orbit And Landing

Twenty-one hours after entering lunar orbit, Neil Armstrong and Buzz Aldrin would have entered the LM to check the systems for a descent to the lunar surface. After separating from the CSM, the LM - with Neil Armstrong and Buzz Aldrin onboard - would then be put into an elliptical orbit with a pericynthion or low point of 50,000 feet above the Moon. From here the LM using its 10,000-pound thrust engine, would have begun its descent for its touchdown on the lunar surface with Michael Collins remaining in the CSM in lunar orbit.

After touchdown on the lunar surface on July 20, 1969, the crew would have prepared the LM for immediate ascent and then they would have rested for several hours before depressurizing it for their extravehicular activity (EVA). Neil Armstrong was the first to descend the LM ladder and step onto the lunar surface with his now famous quote, "One small step for man, one giant leap for mankind" although there is now some dispute as to what he actually said. However, for the purposes of this chapter, Armstrong's quote is close enough.

Armstrong and Aldrin would spend a total of 22 hours on the lunar surface, with approximately two of those hours for EVA. Of these two hours, they setup a couple of scientific experiments and collected lunar samples that were brought back to Earth, as well as many photos and videos of their EVA on the Moon.

Lunar Liftoff

After Armstrong and Aldrin completed their EVA, they then prepared to leave the lunar surface. The LM had two basic components, the descent stage and the ascent stage. The descent stage encompassed the landing portion of the LM along with a 10,000-pound thrust engine. The ascent stage had its own 3,500-pound thrust engine. On liftoff from the lunar surface, the ascent stage of the LM separated from the descent stage, using it as a launching pad and leaving it behind on the lunar surface.

Figure 1.4 – Apollo 11 Lunar Module after landing on the lunar surface, crew member working and Apollo 17 liftoff Source: NASA

After liftoff from the lunar surface, the LM docked with the CM 3 ½ hours later. Once the LM docked with the CM, all lunar samples and videos were stowed onboard the CM and the LM ascent stage was jettisoned from the CM. The latter would then have moved onto its Trans Earth Insertion (TEI) for its three-day voyage back. Again, the Apollo 11 spacecraft would have been put into PTC and three midcourse corrections were planned. The midcourse correction aspect of the mission will be analyzed in detail in Chapter 3.

Back To Earth And Splashdown

Once Apollo 11 had reached Earth, the CM would have separated from the Service Module and begun its re-entry procedure by positioning the aft part to enter Earth's atmosphere first. This aft portion of the CM contained the main heat shield needed to protect the astronauts and the CM from burning up due to friction with the Earth's atmosphere.

Figure 1.5 – Artist impression of Apollo Command Module re-entering Earth's atmosphere
Source: Wikimedia

Apollo 11 would have entered Earth's atmosphere at 400,000 feet at 36,194 feet per second. The CM splashed down in the Pacific Ocean approximately 1000 miles southwest of Honolulu at approximately 12:50 pm EDT, July 24, 1969.

Figure 1.6 – Apollo 11 splashdown
Source: NASA

All of this of course, is according to the official records. But there are many unanswered questions and contradictions regarding the Apollo manned Moon missions, some of which will be discussed in this book starting with the Saturn V.

---

* All of the facts pertaining to the official narrative in this chapter have been taken from the NASA press kit which can be purchased from Amazon.com.

Chapter Two

The Saturn V Rocket

L.E.O., Far As We Go!

The space program was moved to the forefront of the United States' foreign policy when the government was caught off guard by the launch of the first artificial satellite in the world, Sputnik, to Low Earth Orbit (LEO), by the former Soviet Union on October 4, 1957. This mission was followed by Sputnik 2, launched November 3, 1957 and Sputnik 3, launched May 15, 1958. In fact, when it came to the space program, unmanned or manned, the Soviets were first in almost everything.

For example, they were the first to:

- Have satellites in LEO.
- Have a man-made object pass near the Moon.
- Launch animals to LEO.
- Launch the first man to LEO.
- Launch a dual manned mission to LEO.
- Launch the first woman to LEO.
- Launch a multi-person crew of three to LEO.
- Have an astronaut leave his space capsule, while in LEO.

- Land a probe on the Moon's surface and transmit from there.

- Rendezvous and dock an unmanned spacecraft in LEO.

- Send small animals to the Moon and back, apparently unharmed.

- Rendezvous and dock between two manned spacecraft in LEO for an exchange of crews.

As is apparent, the Soviets were well ahead in the space race with their numerous accomplishments. In fact, for thirty years (from 1957 to 1987) they were first in just about everything when it came to their space program; everything, that is, except having accomplished the first manned landing on the Moon. Today (as of 2018), theirs is the only country in the world with a working manned spacecraft capable of launching astronauts to LEO to exchange crews with the International Space Station (ISS).

These Soviet 'firsts' prompted the American government to come up with an ambitious plan for gaining superiority over the Soviet space program. This of course led to President John F. Kennedy's speech to Congress in 1961, proposing to send a manned mission to the Moon and return the astronaut safely to Earth, before the end of that decade. So, the American government had to achieve this monumental goal in just eight years, with technology that didn't exist at the time. Also, given the political climate during the Cold War, superiority was the goal, which meant that hubris, not a genuine drive for scientific enquiry, drove both the American and the Soviet space program policies.

The first man to reach space was the Soviet cosmonaut Yuri Gagarin, with Vostok 1, which was launched on April 12, 1961. Gagarin subsequently became the first man to orbit the Earth, in 108 minutes, during which he reached an orbital altitude of 203 miles. The first American to reach space was Alan Shepard, with the Mercury mission launched on May 5, 1961. Shepard's mission was a 15-minute suborbital flight reaching a height of 116 miles. Evidently the American space program had a lot of catching up to do.

Figure 2.1- Yuri Gagarin
Source: Wikimedia

After Alan Shepard's mission, John Glenn became the first American to orbit the Earth, with the second Mercury mission, launched February 20, 1962, almost a year after Yuri Gagarin's historic first orbital mission. Glen stayed in LEO for almost five hours.

Figure 2.2 - Alan Shepard and John Glenn
Source: Wikimedia

NASA continued with its manned Mercury space program until 1963. It was almost two years before the first manned launch of its second space program, with the Gemini missions, which then ended in 1966. The purpose of these manned missions was to learn and perfect techniques in preparation for the Apollo Moon missions. Further, as the technology evolved with these missions, so did spacecraft capacity, where the:

- Mercury missions was a one-man crew
- Gemini missions, a two-man crew, and
- Apollo missions, a three-man crew

It became obvious in the Mercury and Gemini missions that automation was a necessary component in any manned mission in LEO or beyond. Astronauts quickly realized that success in these missions had less to do with their flying skills as military pilots and more to do with automation and the increased need for more sophisticated computer systems. As you'll learn in Chapter 3, the computer systems on the Apollo missions were nowhere near the technology that would have been needed for a successful manned mission traveling 240,000 miles to the Moon and the same distance back.

After the end of the Gemini manned missions, NASA continued with the Apollo program, which launched the first:

- Unmanned Saturn IB on February 26, 1966
- Manned Saturn IB, with Apollo 7 on October 11, 1968
- Unmanned Saturn V on November 9, 1967

The next mission in the Apollo program was the launch of the third Saturn V on December 21, 1968, which was the first manned mission of a Saturn V and the first manned mission to circumnavigate the Moon. So, in less than eight years, NASA had managed to not only match the Soviet space program, but surpass Soviet accomplishments in the space race to achieve what has been called the greatest scientific achievement of the 20th century, with the first manned landing on the Moon's surface, with Apollo 11, on July 20, 1969.

In the next section, I've provided a brief history of the scientists recruited into NASA and one of the most important contributors to the design and manufacture of the Saturn V rocket.

The Apollo Saturn V Program

The Apollo program was implemented in order to meet President Kennedy's goal of landing a man on the Moon by the end of the 1960s. This required new and innovative technologies to design and manufacture a heavy lift rocket, which ultimately became known as the Saturn V. This new design was needed to launch the hardware necessary for a manned lunar landing.

The Saturn V was reportedly the most powerful heavy lift rocket ever built, which produced a combined total of over 7.5 million pounds of thrust in its five F-1 engines located in the first stage of the Saturn V. There has been no working heavy lift rocket capable of this power output since the end of the

Apollo Moon missions. It apparently functioned virtually flawlessly during the Apollo program from 1969 to 1972. In 1973, NASA decided that it would be cost-efficient to design a reusable vehicle, replacing the Saturn V, which was supposed to have been proven technology. Subsequently the Saturn V program was canceled after launching the first American space station, Skylab, on May 14, 1973. After several years without a manned space vehicle, NASA launched its first reusable manned spacecraft, the Space Shuttle, on April 12, 1981, twenty years to the day since Yuri Gagarin became the first person to orbit the Earth. However, due to claims of cost inefficiencies and overruns, the Space Shuttle program was also cancelled in 2011. As of today, NASA no longer has a working manned space vehicle capable of launch to LEO.

History

The Saturn V rocket program's origins go back to World War II (WWII) and the German rocket program, with its Vengeance Weapon 1 aeroplane (V-1) and the Vengeance Weapon 2 rocket (V-2). The V-2 was the first ballistic missile ever built and was used to terrorize London in WWII. The architect of the V-1 and V-2 was Wernher von Braun, reportedly a brilliant aerospace engineer who, as history records, was secretly moved to the United States from Germany at the end of WWII by the American Office of Strategic Services (OSS), under its program, Operation Paperclip. The OSS was the predecessor to the Central Intelligence Agency (CIA). It is estimated that the OSS recruited 1,600 German scientists, engineers, and technicians, while the Soviets recruited an estimated 2,000 German scientists. Wernher von Braun and other German scientists worked for the U.S. army on its intermediate-range ballistic missile (IRBM) program. Later, von Braun and his group were absorbed into the newly formed space agency, NASA.

Wernher von Braun And His Alleged War Crimes

Two years before WWII, Germany had moved their rocket technology to Peenemunde, a rocket base located on the island of Usedom, on the Peene River, off the Baltic coast. However, after WWII began, allied forces launched air raids on Peenemunde, as a result of which this technology, along with the technicians, were moved to other bases around the country, like the underground rocket base at the Mittelwerk plant. Serious allegations, amounting to war crimes against humanity, have been made about personnel of that particular facility, including Wernher von Braun, who was a member of the Nazi party.

During WWII, Germany was using concentration camp prisoners as slave laborers at their Mittelwerk plant. An estimated 20,000 slave laborers died from starvation, physical abuse, executions, and brutal working conditions. There has been plenty of debate over the decades about Wernher von Braun's involvement in the estimated 20,000 deaths of war prisoners used as slaves, and the deplorable and hellish conditions they had to endure.

Wikipedia:

> SS General Hans Kammler, who as an engineer had constructed several concentration camps, including Auschwitz, had a reputation for brutality and had originated the idea of using concentration camp prisoners as slave laborers in the rocket program. Arthur Rudolph, chief engineer of the V-2 rocket at Peenemunde, endorsed this idea in April 1943 when a labor shortage developed. More people died building the V-2 rockets than were killed by it as a weapon. Von Braun admitted visiting the plant at Mittlewerk on many occasions, and called conditions at the plant "repulsive", but claimed never to have witnessed any

deaths or beatings, although it had become clear to him by 1944 that deaths had occurred. He denied ever having visited the Mittelbau-Dora concentration camp itself, where 20,000 died from illness, beatings, and intolerable working conditions.

There were investigations of some of the scientists recruited by the American government, and it is believed that von Braun himself was questioned about what he knew of the conditions at Mittelbau-Dora concentration camp. However, all of these scientists' records were expunged by the OSS when they were recruited by the United States, practically ending any paper trail implicating these German scientists, including von Braun. The CIA has maintained that secrecy although, as the above quote shows, it's now more of an open secret. There were supposedly some witnesses that testified on behalf of von Braun, saying he tried to better working conditions for the slaved laborers when possible. However, the veracity of these witnesses and their statements should be considered first, before coming to any conclusions.

As for Wernher von Braun's Nazi affiliation, proponents of the Apollo missions say that 'conspiracy theorists' use this fact to promote the Apollo mission hoax story. Most serious researchers, who believe these missions to have been faked, separate von Braun's Nazi affiliation and acknowledge his purported brilliance in rocket technology. However, there is a limit as to how far that technology will go. Likewise, serious proponents of the Apollo missions also acknowledge von Braun's Nazi affiliation, along with his purported brilliance in rocket technology.

Figure 2.3 - Wernher von Braun
Source: Wikimedia

This book won't investigate von Braun's background and alleged war crimes further, as there is much more information available in other books and online. However, it is important to mention von Braun's background and possible history of war crimes, to put the Apollo missions' program into its proper context.

In the next section, the listings of the Apollo mission series are provided, as they are integral to the understanding of the questionable practices of NASA's testing involving the Saturn IB and the Saturn V.

The Apollo Saturn Rocket Series Starts With Tragedy

After being recruited into the newly formed space agency, NASA, Wernher von Braun was appointed as the director of the Marshall Space Flight Center (MSFC) and as chief architect of the Saturn V rocket. The Apollo program started with the first launch in 1961, involving a variation of the Saturn V rocket, leading up to the first manned mission to land on the lunar surface in 1969. However, when trying to explain each mission and its progress, Apollo mission nomenclature gets a little complicated. For example, the first mission in the series was Saturn Apollo 1 (SA-1), not to be confused with Apollo 1, which was a mission simulation of a launch that ended in tragedy, killing three astronauts. There are also the Apollo missions with the prefix AS (not to be confused with SA). To further complicate things, NASA had internal and external designations for each mission. Apparently, the external designations were for the media. In addition, there is a series of three books by Eugen Reichl listing each mission in the Apollo program in chronological order, which helps to clarify the Apollo mission's nomenclature.

It is the actual Saturn 1B and, most of all, the Saturn V, which interests us, since these two Saturn variations involved the first manned mission of the Apollo program to LEO, to circumnavigate the Moon, and to land on the lunar surface.

Leading up to and including Apollo 11, there were 30 missions in the Apollo program. Of these 30 missions, 21 missions involved a variation of the Saturn rocket. Of these 21 missions, five were the Saturn IB and six were the Saturn V. However, Apollo 4, the 23rd mission, is where the actual Saturn V missions leading up to Apollo 11 began. Apollo 4 was the first unmanned launch of the Saturn V, but a commonly asked question is: what happened to Apollos 1, 2, and 3? Did they involve the Saturn IB? No, they didn't even involve a launch and in fact, this is part of what leads to some of the confusion with these Apollo missions. In order to better answer these questions, let's discuss each mission in chronological order, starting with the Apollo 1 tragedy.

> **Apollo 1:** On January 27, 1967, at 1:30 pm, Commander Virgil "Gus" Grissom; Senior Pilot Edward White and Command Module Pilot Roger Chaffee entered the Apollo 1 Command Module (CM) on top of the Saturn IB for a

launch simulation. All three astronauts were in spacesuits and when they were strapped into their seats, the escape tower's protective cover was lowered into position on the CM and locked. The astronauts were, for all intents and purposes, sealed in. Several hours into the launch simulation, at approximately 6:30 pm, a fire broke out within the CM. While the astronauts were yelling frantically over the communications frequency and desperately trying to open the CM hatch, technicians outside also tried to do the same, but to no avail. The heat around the CM was far too intense for the technicians to get close. By the time the technicians opened the hatch, Virgil "Gus" Grissom, Edward White, and Roger Chaffee had been incinerated. This launch simulation was in preparation for the first manned mission of the Saturn IB, with Grissom, White and Chaffee. This simulation mission was then designated, posthumously, as Apollo 1, in honour of the lost crew.

There have been lots of discussions over the decades about this tragedy, as well as some serious accusations levelled at NASA about possible foul play. One theory suggests that Gus Grissom, who more than hinted that the Apollo program was plagued with problems and that it was years away from any attempt at a manned lunar landing, needed to be silenced. However, rather than speculate on this serious allegation, let's instead look at the facts.

Gus Grissom was known to be outspoken and was increasingly becoming frustrated with the numerous anomalies with the Apollo program. In a press conference shortly before the tragedy, Grissom hung a lemon on the outside of the CM for the whole world to see, the inference being that the CM was a "lemon", and not fit for manned space missions.

As was common practice with the Mercury and Gemini manned space programs, the CM was filled with over-pressurized pure oxygen. Since oxygen makes up about 20% of our nitrogen-oxygen atmosphere, there is enough outside atmospheric pressure at sea level for the lungs to absorb that oxygen into the bloodstream. However, to duplicate sea level pressure in spacecraft in LEO would require engineering the hull of the capsule strong enough to withstand sea level pressure against the vacuum of space, as well as carrying the required amount of nitrogen and oxygen tanks to regulate the mixture. Reinforcement of the CM hull, as well as extra nitrogen and oxygen tanks, would have added weight to the spacecraft, which means more engine power for launch that translates into more propellant and therefore more expense.

In order to keep costs down, NASA decided to use a pure oxygenated atmosphere and regulate the oxygen environment in the spacecraft to lower levels than that of sea level pressure, but with the oxygen pressure content higher, making the transfer of oxygen from the lungs to the bloodstream possible while in orbit. This proved deadly during the simulated launch of Apollo 1, when a spark inside the complex design of the CM caused a fire, turning the over-pressurized pure oxygen environment into a torch, killing the three astronauts onboard. After the tragic incident, NASA changed the CM environment to 60% oxygen and 40% nitrogen on launch, which decreased slowly on ascent to an eventual pure oxygenated environment over the next day.

North American Aviation (NAA) was the primary contractor for the Command Module. NAA inspector Thomas Baron had submitted a 500-page report and testified to Congress on April 21, 1967, regarding the anomalies leading up to the Apollo 1 tragedy. Six days later, Thomas Baron, his wife and his stepdaughter were killed instantly when a train crashed into their car. Since then, Thomas' 500-page report to Congress has disappeared.

You can find NASA's Internal Review Report detailing its findings on its website, but there was nothing conclusive as to the actual cause of the Apollo 1 tragedy. However, the report does make for some disturbing reading.

> It seems that no-one had seriously considered the hazards of an over-pressurized cabin full of pure oxygen.[1]

Wikipedia:

> In the first episode of the 2009 documentary series NASA: Triumph and Tragedy, Jim McDivitt said that NASA had no idea how a 100% oxygenated atmosphere would influence burning. Similar remarks by other astronauts were expressed in the 2007 documentary film In the Shadow of the Moon.

These two understated quotes delineate the 'expertise' of NASA personnel involved in the Apollo program, who were seemingly ignorant to the dangers of an over-pressurized oxygenated environment.

Note to NASA: It has been established throughout millennia that depriving fires of oxygen is a very effective way of putting fires out. Common sense should then dictate that a pure oxygenated environment is not only a fire hazard, it's a blowtorch waiting for a spark.

Figure 2.4 – Exterior and Interior view of the Apollo 1 Tragedy
Source: Wikimedia

- **Apollos 2 & 3**: After the Apollo 1 tragedy, Apollo 2 was assigned to a previous mission, AS-202, and Apollo 3 was assigned to AS-203. Therefore, the very existence of Apollos 2 and 3 is up for discussion.

Now let's look at Apollos 4 to 11 and, as you read on, pay close attention to the first manned mission of the Saturn V.

- **Apollo 4:** This was the 23rd mission and the first to involve a Saturn V, which was an unmanned mission launched from Cape Canaveral on November 9, 1967. It was a LEO mission. Duration of this mission was nine hours.

- **Apollo 5:** This was the 24th mission and the fourth to involve a Saturn IB, which was an unmanned mission launched on January 22, 1968. It was the first mission to test an unmanned Lunar Module (LM) in LEO, but it should be noted that this particular LM was structurally incomplete. Therefore, this doesn't qualify as a test of the LM in the actual conditions of spaceflight. Duration of this mission was 11 hours.

- **Apollo 6**: This was the 25th mission and the second to involve a Saturn V, another unmanned mission launched on April 4, 1968. It was a LEO mission. This mission had significant problems with its five F-1 engines. Duration of this mission was 10 hours.

- **Apollo 7:** The was the 26th mission, the fifth to involve the Saturn IB and the first manned Apollo mission, launched on October 11, 1968. Its mission was to test the CM and Service Module (SM) in the actual conditions of space in LEO. Duration of this mission was 11 days.

- **Apollo 8**: This was the 27th mission, launched on December 8, 1968. This mission should be considered the most significant for three reasons, as it was the first manned:

  - Launch of a Saturn V,
  - Mission to leave LEO, and
  - Mission to circumnavigate the Moon.

  Up to the launch of Apollo 8, the Saturn V had a combined total of only 19 hours of experience in the actual conditions of spaceflight, and yet this mission was reported to have been flawless. Duration of this mission was six days.

- **Apollo 9:** This was the 28th mission, the fourth to involve the Saturn V and the second manned mission of that vehicle, launched on March 3, 1969. This was the second mission to involve the LM and the first manned mission involving that vehicle. However, this LM should be considered the first test in the conditions of spaceflight, since it was a structurally complete version of that vehicle. Duration of this mission was 10 days.

- **Apollo 10:** This was the 29th mission, the fifth to involve the Saturn V and the third manned mission of that vehicle, launched on May 18, 1969. It was the second manned mission to leave LEO to circumnavigate the Moon. It was also the second manned mission of the LM. While in lunar orbit, the LM separated from the CM. The LM descended to within 50,000 feet of the lunar surface, and then aborted the descent to rendezvous and dock back with the CM. This mission was supposed to have been a test run for Apollo 11. Duration of this mission was eight days.

- **Apollo 11:** This was the 30th mission, the sixth to involve the Saturn V and the fourth manned mission of that vehicle, launched on July 16, 1969. It was the third manned mission to leave LEO to circumnavigate the Moon and involved the first manned lunar landing. Duration of this mission was eight days (See Chapter 1 for details).

The program continued with Apollos 12, 13, 14, 15, 16 and 17, but the focus of this chapter are the missions leading up to and including Apollo 11.

Note: From the 23rd mission on, the duration of each mission of the Apollo series has been rounded off. For the exact durations of these missions, see NASA's website at www.nasa.gov.

When one actually studies the details of the Apollo program, it can be seen that, aside from the testing of the different components of the Saturn rocket on the ground, there was a minimal amount of testing done of a functional Saturn IB and Saturn V in the actual conditions of spaceflight before the first manned missions of those vehicles.

However, before I talk about the minimal testing of the Saturn V, we must discuss one of the most important aspects of the

Saturn V, i.e. the 'powerful' F-1 engines. The F-1 engines were an integral part of the Saturn V, necessary for the success of an Apollo Moon landing mission and, as you'll learn in the next section, the power output from these engines of the Saturn V were overrated. In layman's terms, low F-1 engine power means no Apollo Moon landings.

The Overrated Power Of The Saturn V F-1 Engines

Studies by scientists and engineers outside of the western engineering and scientific communities that question any aspect of the Apollo missions are usually not published in western scientific journals or magazines and are, for the most part, ignored. However, it's not so easy to ignore the work of these scientists: Gennady Icvhenkov, Ph.D., Alexander Popov, Ph.D., Andrei Bulatov and S. G. Pokrovsky, Ph.D., as their work disputes the claims by NASA on the performance of the Saturn V, in particular the F-1 engines.

The concept of the powerful F-1 engine was actually initiated by the Air Force in the 1950s. However, after President Dwight D. Eisenhower established NASA on July 29, 1958, NASA assumed responsibility for the F-1 engine and awarded the contract for design and production to Rocketdyne.

One of the main differences between the Saturn IB and the Saturn V was their lift capabilities. The first stage of the Saturn V contained five F-1 engines, the second stage contained five J-2 engines, and the third stage contained one J-2 engine.

The F-1 engines gave the Saturn V its heavy lift capabilities and the needed power to propel a significant payload, as in the launch of the hardware necessary for a manned landing on the Moon. Without the F-1 engines, the Apollo Moon missions could not have happened and, in fact, that is exactly what was claimed by a former Rocketdyne employee, Bill Kaysing over 40 years ago. Now, there are new claims questioning the power output of the F-1 engines. Bill Kaysing, and these new claims, will be discussed in detail below.

Figure 2.5 – F-1 Engines of the Saturn V
Source: Wikimedia

Minimal Testing Of The F-1 Engines

Rocketdyne had done static testing of the F-1 engines, but it's difficult to ascertain just how many of these static tests were done. I contacted the MSFC for documents regarding static tests of the F-1 engine and was provided with a link to their technical documents. I searched through 300 documents and found one about the F-1 engine, but nothing as to the number of static tests that were conducted. I contacted the National Archives but got no precise information there either. I then decided to contact Rocketdyne, now called Aerojet Rocketdyne, when I found www.thespacereview.com.

Their stated purpose:

> The Space Review is an online publication devoted to in-depth articles, commentary, and reviews regarding all aspects of space exploration: science, technology, policy, business, and more.

A posted article on their website about the F-1 engine has this to say:

> The longstanding story that NASA lost or destroyed the Saturn 5 plans quickly falls to pieces when one learns about the F-1 Production Knowledge Retention Program. This was a project at Rocketdyne, the company that built the F-1 engine, to preserve as much technical documentation and knowledge about the engine as was possible. According to an inventory of records, this produced about twenty volumes of material on topics such as the engine's injector ring set, valves, engine assembly, and checkout and thermal insulation and electrical cables, among others.[2]

In fact, "lost or destroyed" Saturn V documents only add to the suspicions that NASA is hiding something, since these are the very rockets that used the F-1 engines. The author of the article, Dwayne A. Day, then says the goal was "to preserve as much technical documentation and knowledge about the F-1 engines as was possible." If that was the case, why not preserve all of it?

Day then describes the testing of the F-1 engine:

> Rocketdyne delivered 98 production engines to NASA, of which 65 were launched. A total of 56 equivalent development engines were tested. The company conducted 2,771 production and R&D firing tests of single engines, 1,110 total full duration tests, and

accumulated 239,124 seconds – over 66 hours – of engine firing experience. The five-engine cluster used on the Saturn 5 was fired at the Mississippi and Alabama test facilities 34 times, with 18 full duration tests for a total of 15,534 seconds of engine experience. Rocketdyne estimated in 1992 that the F-1 engine development program had cost $1.77 billion dollars in FY91 dollars. [3]

Dwayne Day also used large numbers to emphasize that there were many tests of the F-1 engines which when translated:

- The combined "production and R&D firing tests" of single engines and full duration tests of the F-1 engines, was over 66 hours.
- The five-engine cluster tests of the F-1 engines, was four hours in total.

There was a combined total of 70 hours of static tests of the F-1 engines, which seems adequate, given the duration of each five-engine cluster after launch (purportedly used in all Apollo missions), which was approximately two minutes. This included 34 five-engine cluster tests, 18 of which were full duration tests. However, the amount of static testing means little or nothing, unless there is comparable testing of the F-1 engines in actual spaceflight conditions, which is equally, if not more important for evaluating engine performance and as you'll see below, testing in the unmanned Saturn V missions, was nowhere near standards and where minimal to say the least.

But before we discuss the overall testing of the F-1 engines in spaceflight conditions, we take a look at some disturbing testing practices before these engines were assigned to a particular mission. I have chosen these four missions for their historical significance in the Apollo program to highlight this:

Apollo 4:

> The First test firing was on February 17, and the programmed duration of just under 41 seconds met all test objectives. Another test was conducted on February 25, but a red-line observer reacted to an incorrect reading by ending the test 83.2 seconds into the planned duration of 128 seconds. The incorrect reading proved to be due to a faulty transducer. After analysis of the results, it was decided that a full duration test would not be needed. S-IC-1 was refurbished, subjected to a number of inspections and checks by MSFC's laboratories, loaded on to the sea-going barge Poseidon and shipped to KSC. It became the first stage of AS-501, which was launched unmanned as Apollo 4 on November 9, 1967.[4]

The first test firing of these F-1 engines for Apollo 4 was conducted on February 17 and 25, 1966. These F-1 engines were then stored at the Kennedy Space Center (KSC) for a year and eight months before they were used on Apollo 4, and that is without any further testing of these engines. This mission seemingly worked flawlessly.

Apollo 6:

> S-IC-2 was installed in the Static Test Stand at MSFC in May, 1966. The first test firing, on June 7, 1966, lasted for 123.3 seconds. However, of the F-1 engines on this stage, F-4017 showed thrust anomalies. After being removed it was inspected, refurbished and subjected to three further individual tests, during which it functioned satisfactorily. It was reinstalled on S-IC-2 in August. Refurbishment, inspection and checkout of the stage by several of MSFC's laboratories took several months. It was then loaded aboard the barge

> Poseidon, shipped to KSC in March 1967, and became the first stage of AS-502, which was launched, unmanned, as Apollo 6. [5]

Apollo 6 was launched April 4, 1968, almost two years after the last recorded test of its F-1 engines. This mission experienced problems with its F-1 engines during launch, which will be discussed in detail further below.

Apollo 8:

> The first S-IC to be manufactured by Boeing at the Michoud Assembly Facility in Louisiana was S-IC-3, and it was the final stage tested at MSFC. It was shipped by the barge Poseidon from Michoud to MSFC and placed on the Static Test Stand on October 3, 1966. The first test, on November 15, 1966 lasted for 121.7 seconds. The stage was removed from the stand on November 21 and returned to Michoud. After refurbishment, engineering change orders and system checks, NASA accepted it for shipment to KSC. On arrival there, on December 27, 1967, it was placed in storage. It became the first stage of AS-503, which was to be the third unmanned test flight of the Saturn V, but when this was cancelled the vehicle was used for Apollo 8, the first manned mission, which flew out to orbit around the Moon. [6]

The F-1 engines were stored for over a year without any further testing before they were used to launch Apollo 8. And in just seven months, the problems that plagued Apollo 6 were resolved, before the first manned mission of Apollo 8, which was seemingly flawless.

Apollo 11:

> On March 1, 1968, S-IC-6 arrived at the Mississippi Test Facility on the barge Pearl River. It was installed in the B-2 stand on March 4 and subjected to months of checkout and tests. Finally, on August 13, it was fired for the planned 125 seconds. All five F-1 engines performed within their performance parameters. This test was particularly significant due to the inclusion of the 'pogo' suppression system, added after Apollo 6 suffered from this longitudinal oscillation when launched on April 4. Following the post-firing checks, the stage was returned to Michoud on August 28 for refurbishment, modification and checkout. On 16 February, 1969, it was loaded onto the barge Orion for shipment to KSC, where it arrived four days later. S-IC-6 is perhaps the most historically significant of the Saturn V first stages because it was stacked as SA-506 and launched as Apollo 11, the mission that achieved Kennedy's challenge of landing men on the Moon. [7]

It seems there were no more test firings of the F-1 engines after August 1968, before they were installed for the Apollo 11 mission, which was touted to be the most historically significant mission in the Apollo program, as well as the greatest scientific achievement of the 20th century.

The previous four quotes are from the same book on the F-1 engine. In a review of that book, Jeff Foust had this to say:

> Young relies on a combination of primary sources, including NASA and Rocketdyne documents, as well as oral interviews with people who worked on the F-1, who provide additional insights and anecdotes that can't be found in the original documentation. [8]

Contrary to what Dwayne A. Day has said regarding the "F-1 Production Knowledge Retention Program," it's apparent that, decades later, it's up to people who worked on the F-1 engines to fill in the missing data from incomplete documents. Further, as mentioned earlier, it is the "lost or destroyed" Saturn V documents that are needed to substantiate any of the data related to the F-1 engine static tests.

In addition, NASA knew in the early 1960s that the F-1 engines were not up to the task of launching the required Apollo hardware for a manned lunar landing, as explained in the next section.

Former Rocketdyne Employee Bill Kaysing Exposes The F-1 Fraud

The first person to expose the F-1 fraud, and simultaneously the Apollo Moon hoax, was Bill Kaysing, who published a book on it in 1976. Bill Kaysing was an employee of Rocketdyne and had direct access to documents pertaining to the F-1 engine tests. He was an employee of Rocketdyne from 1956 to 1963, a period which coincides with the first static tests of the F-1 engine.

Wikipedia:

> Kaysing began work as the senior technical writer at Rocketdyne, starting on February 13, 1956. On September 24, 1956, he became a service analyst; starting September 15, 1958, he worked as a service engineer; and starting on October 10, 1962, as a publications analyst. On May 31, 1963, he resigned for personal reasons.
>
> Trained as neither an engineer nor a specialist, he nevertheless also served as the company's head of

technical publications, during his time from 1956 to 1963 at Rocketdyne (a division of North American Aviation and from 1967 of Rockwell International) where Saturn V rocket engines were designed and built.

Bill Kaysing's decision to resign from Rocketdyne had a lot to do with what he saw in the F-1 engine documents. And aside from the fact that Kaysing was not trained as an "engineer nor a specialist," as Wikipedia is quick to point out, it's apparent that Rocketdyne was impressed enough with his expertise to hire him to analyze reports. It follows that Kaysing was more than qualified to read technical documents and evaluate data regarding the F-1 engines.

During his employment at Rocketdyne, Kaysing claims to have seen evidence in these documents that the F-1 engines of the Saturn V were not capable of producing the power output needed to launch the Apollo hardware into LEO for the lunar missions. This is significant since NASA, after much debate, adopted the method of Lunar Orbital Rendezvous (LOR) for a lunar landing, which required NASA to launch the Apollo lunar hardware as well as the astronauts in one mission, as opposed to launching the lunar hardware in a separate mission. This of course would have required the purported heavy lift capabilities of the F-1 engines in the Saturn V.

Kaysing has been criticized and ridiculed over the decades, and sometimes in less obvious ways, as with the Wikipedia quote above. However, Kaysing was never deterred and for the last several decades he maintained his claims that the real power output on the F-1 engines was far less than NASA claimed.

Bill Kaysing writes:

> From the date of the decision to simulate, a modified hardware program was conducted. For example, the Saturn C-5 Moon rocket assembly was built to

specifications with one major modification: instead of totally unreliable F-1 engines, five booster engines of the more dependable B-1 type as used in the C-1 cluster for the Atlas missile were used.

Although a cluster of B-1 engines produced only one-half of the output of a single F-1 chamber, the power (750,000 pounds of thrust) was sufficient to launch the virtually empty Apollo vehicle. If the rocket had been in its designed form it would have weighed 6,000,000 pounds, or 3,000 tons fully loaded. This is the weight of a U.S. naval destroyer, further pointing out the total impracticality of the venture. However, by eliminating every aspect of the moon voyage – fuel, heavy machines, LEM vehicles, etc., the total weight of the modified, short-range, simulated voyage Apollo was less than one-twentieth of the original, or about 150 tons. This loading was well within the capabilities of the B-1 propulsion units. Also, since the originally planned two million parts were reduced to a mere 150,000 gadgets, the success of the limited mission was virtually assured.

However, even the C-1 Atlas engines were known to explode on the pad or shortly following launch. Thus, the escape module for the astronauts was left intact and functioning. If there had been an accidental loss of thrust or other mishap, it would have been simple to have the "saved" astronauts merge from the escape module after its recovery.[9]

Note: To clarify, the C-5 was eventually changed to the Saturn V.

Bill Kaysing may have gotten some of the details in his book wrong, for example the actual mechanics of the modified Saturn V, but his overall point that the F-1 engines did not have the heavy lift capabilities has recently been substantiated by the previously mentioned scientists, Ivchenkov, Popov, Bulatov and Pokrovsky.

It's obvious that what Bill Kaysing initially saw in these F-1 documents, was either deleted from the record or the original documents have gone missing. And since the power output of the Saturn V F-1 engines were not what NASA had claimed, then by inference NASA fabricated future documents, that is, if any of this data even existed.

Engineer Gennady Ivchenkov Ph.D., Substantiates Bill Kaysing's Claims

Gennady Ivchenkov published a 55-page article on the performance of the F-1 engine. His premise is that the combustion chamber of the F-1 engine was unstable, meaning that the F-1 engine could not have used its full power potential.

Gennady Ivchenkov writes:

> The question of whether the Saturn V rocket engines corresponded to NASA's stated characteristics is directly related to the 'Apollo Moon hoax' – did the Americans really go to the Moon in 1969-1972, or was it an elaborate hoax?
>
> This question was raised initially by the Americans themselves almost immediately after the Apollo missions. Over the years, a considerable amount of direct and indirect evidence has come to light, that at least some of the missions were in fact staged.[10]

One of the aspects of this indirect evidence Ivchenkov talks about, is NASA's marketing publications, in which Chief Designers of the Soviet Space industry had no trouble deciphering that the actual power output of the F-1 engines was not as NASA claimed. Further, as Ivchenkov says, it is only recently that documents have become available that contradict the claims made by NASA. So, it seems some of the original data for the F-1 engines did exist and did survive, validating Bill Kaysing's claims.

For the general public, there are sources of information in technical books and articles detailing the different aspects of the Saturn V and its F-1 engines. However, one should be cautious as to the reliability of any of the data in these sources.

> Regarding quotations, all technical information in North America (including technical guidelines, manuals, instructions, etc.) is written by so-called technical writers, who put the available material into literary form accessible to the public. It's just a job, something like a journalist writing on technical subjects. It is easy to distort the source material (several inconsistencies in the F-1 records are noted later in this article). Therefore, all numbers and technical details in such documents should be treated with caution.[11]

Note: Many journalists have written on technical matters and have done so accurately by accessing documents when necessary. However, it would be incumbent on the reader to carefully check the financial backing and sources of any of the numerous investigative journalists who publish such material. Proponents of the Apollo missions are quick to point out that these documents can be accessed at various online sites, such as MSFC, NASA and The National Archives. But many of these documents are incomplete or are missing. And any of these documents that still exist, could easily be translated and published in books, placed in public libraries, as well as being stored away, e.g. in the National Archives. Also, a lot of these technical books are based on interviews conducted decades later with personnel who were involved with the Apollo missions and rely more on memory, since documents are either incomplete or missing.

Regarding the F-1 thrust chamber:

> The thrust chamber body provides a combustion chamber for burning propellants to generate pressure, and an expansion nozzle to expel the combustion gases at high velocity to produce thrust.[12]

The combustion chamber of the F-1 engine produced thrust nearly ten times greater than any previous rocket engine. The temperature of the combustion chamber extension reached 5,900 degrees Fahrenheit and thus, needed to be cooled. The material that cooled the combustion chamber was provided by tubes running along the combustion chamber walls. The tubing material needed to be strong enough to withstand the thrust force, yet light enough to minimize the overall weight of the Saturn V.

> Fuel enters the fuel inlet manifold through two inlets set 180 degrees apart. From the manifold, 70 percent of the fuel is diverted through 89 alternating corrosion-resistant steel 'down' tubes the length of the chamber. A manifold at the nozzle exit returns the fuel through the remaining 89 'up' tubes to supply the injector. The fuel flowing through the tubes provides regenerative cooling of the chamber walls during engine operation.[13]

It is the material used to make these tubes that caused the combustion chamber instability.

As the analysis in Ivchenkov's article shows, "The source gives the thickness of the F-1 tubes as 0.457mm, the accuracy of which is highly questionable, since such a wall thickness contradicts the cooling requirements."

The combustion chamber tubes were made of thin-walled tubes of a nickel alloy, Inconel X-750, different from what was used in the seemingly successful H-1 engines in the Saturn IB. As Ivchenkov explains, when using Inconel X-750, this material could not have withstood the pressures and temperatures produced by the F-1 engine thrust. In this case, the combustion chamber thrust would have been throttled back, which means the Saturn V could not have lifted the necessary Apollo hardware into LEO for a manned Moon landing mission. A NASA report regarding a static test of the F-1 engine in 1959, as quoted in Ivchenkov's article, shows that the F-1 did indeed produce the necessary thrust, but with a catch:

> In January 1959, Rocketdyne's NASA contract included requirements for a series of feasibility firings of the new F-1 booster; two months later the engine hinted at its future success with a brief main-stage ignition. The trial run demonstrated stable combustion for 200 milliseconds and achieved a thrust level of 4 500 000 newtons (1 000 000 pounds). In conducting these tests, Rocketdyne used a solid-wall "boiler-plate" thrust chamber and injector-a far cry from flight hardware-but the unheard-of mark of 4 500 000 newtons (1,000,000 pounds) of thrust had been reached by a single engine.[14]

The catch being the sustained static test firing did not match the duration of the Apollo launch up to the separation of the first stage of the Saturn V, which contained the F-1 engines. This is an important point to remember, keeping in mind the actual conditions of spaceflight. This is obviously an example of what Bill Kaysing was talking about, when he stated that these F-1 engine firing tests could not be sustained.

Rocketdyne had built several test facilities for static testing of the F-1 engines. The Bravo stand test facility at Santa Susana Field Laboratory was used for the F-1 components testing. But because of the noise and close proximity to housing, full static tests of the F-1 engines were conducted at the Edwards Field Laboratory, away from civilization and of course, out of sight of the public and the media. And although F-1 engine static tests were subsequently done, that's a "far cry" from actual "flight hardware" and from using a cluster of five F-1 engines in actual spaceflight missions using the Saturn V. It is also difficult to determine or access the power output data of the F-1 engine static tests in the several years leading up to the first Saturn V launch. There was even less testing in actual flight conditions using the F-1 engines in the Saturn V, which will be discussed in the next section.

As has been previously mentioned, Apollo 6, the unmanned second launch of the Saturn V, experienced several problems during its mission.

> Unlike the first launch of the Saturn V, which had been almost flawless, this mission ran into difficulties from the very beginning. The reason was Pogo oscillations, which caused various degrees of damage. During the first stage flight a panel of the payload fairing separated because of vibration and expanding moisture in the structure. While the second stage was operating, failures in fuel lines caused two of the five engines to shut down prematurely, which resulted in the third phase with the payload reaching suboptimal orbit. Instead of the desired circular orbit at 118 miles, it achieved an elliptical orbit with a lowest point of 107 miles.[15]

The above quote gives the impression that it was anything but a fault with the F-1 engines, instead blaming the problem on

Pogo oscillations of the Saturn V. If Apollo 6 had been an actual mission, it would not have been able to proceed on its trajectory to circumnavigate the Moon, given that it did not reach optimal orbit. Further, any attempt to increase its orbit in a last-minute attempt to salvage the mission, would have been out of the question anyway, as the third stage J-2 engine also failed.

In analyzing documents for the J-2 engines as well as photos of the Apollo 6 launch, Ivchenkov observes:

> Various documents and others state that Apollo 6 and Apollo 13 had problems with the J-2 engines on the 2nd and 3rd stages. The J-2 papers mention several cases of cooling tube breakthroughs, but in the available F-1 documents, there is no such information.
>
> At the same time, on the picture of the Apollo 6 flight, it is obvious that one or more F-1 motors of the first stage are burning. Kerosene is leaking, catching fire and forming a huge tail of flame and soot.
>
> Thus, it turns out that NASA, for whatever reason, has not provided complete information about these F-1 problems. Considering that the Apollo 6 damage, essentially related to the design of the F-1 engine, occurred seven months before the Apollo 8 mission, it can be concluded that there was no time for fine-tuning of the engine to the declared characteristics.[16]

NASA has inferred that it was the Pogo oscillations that caused the F-1 engine problems when in fact, it was the opposite; a problem with the F-1 engines caused the Pogo oscillations. But now, we also learn that there were problems with the J-2 engines as well. This is another significant point, since the J-2 engines would have been needed to boost the Saturn V to LEO and the trajectory for a Moon mission.

As further stated in Ivchenkov's article, NASA may have attempted to utilize the full power of the F-1 and J-2 engines with Apollo 6, which led to numerous problems after launch which required the reduction of power to minimize damage and prevent an explosion. The irony here is that it was most likely the design of the tubular cooling system that was responsible for the combustion chamber instability, which prevented the use of full power in the F-1 engines and inevitably prevented an explosion on Apollo 6 during launch. Therefore, for a successful mission, and in the absence of problems experienced with Apollo 6, the initial thrust of the F-1 engines (if they were used) needed to have been throttled back, defeating the F-1 engines' stated purpose, which was to launch the Apollo hardware into LEO for a manned lunar landing mission. Any power in the F-1 engines lower than what NASA has stated would have meant that there were no manned Moon landings, meaning all Apollos missions outside of LEO were faked.

Apparently, after solving the instabilities of the F-1 engine combustion chamber, the actual cause of the problem seems to remain elusive:

> The spontaneous combustion instabilities never reappeared. Until the end, however, the problem was never completely understood. To this day it remains a constant problem in the large rocket engines, for which an individual empirical solution has to be found. To the disappointment of the engineers, a model was never found with which they could generally overcome the problem.[17]

NASA admits it didn't know what caused the problems with the F-1 engines, yet it says the problem was overcome and they worked perfectly during the Apollo missions. However, after 1973, the remaining F-1 engines were never used again.

Note: The issue is not whether the F-1 engines existed or not, as there's evidence that they did and NASA even has the F-1 engines in storage and on display in museums. The issue is whether or not they had the required power output as NASA claims and whether they were used in the Saturn V. The preponderance of the evidence now shows that the F-1 engines didn't have the power output needed to launch the hardware to LEO for a successful manned lunar landing.

The next mission after Apollo 6 using the Saturn V was Apollo 8. As previously mentioned, Apollo 8 was the first manned mission of that vehicle, and the first manned mission to leave LEO to circumnavigate the Moon. All of the problems experienced with Apollo 6 were seemingly solved in just seven months. However, as Ivchenkov points out, seven months would not have given Rocketdyne and NASA enough time to have worked out the problems that were observed with Apollo 6. He further states that Apollo 6 may have actually been the first and last mission of the Saturn V to use the five F-1 engines.

Gennady Ivchenkov concludes:

> The pressure in the F-1 combustion chamber is likely to have been significantly lower than that stated, due to the fundamental shortcomings of the tubular cooling system of American rocket engines. This is further confirmed by the fact that all rocket engines now being developed and currently in use, including those in the United States, use the 'Soviet-style' cooling system."

Consequently, the launch weight of the Saturn V was lower and accordingly could not have ensured the accomplishment of the Apollo Moon landing program.

Nevertheless, although the F-1 engines produced smoke – they worked; they were not exploding in front of the public and were delivering 'something to somewhere'. In general, we can express admiration for the expert Rocketdyne engineers, who managed to get at least some characteristics out of this 'miracle of an American mastermind' (the F-1), as even 500 tons of thrust per chamber is quite a lot.

The true F-1 design and its characteristics, apparently, were significantly different from those stated.[18]

To reiterate: NASA no longer uses a cooling system in its rocket engines that worked seemingly perfectly during the Apollo Moon missions from 1969 – 1972, preferring instead, to use the 'Soviet-style' cooling system.

Alexander Popov Ph.D. And Andrei Bulatov Prove The F-1 Fraud With Apollo 11 Film

As would have been expected, super 8 films by spectators were taken of the Apollo 11 launch. The question is: do any of these old super 8 films still exist? Yes, they do and it is one of these films that was analyzed by Alexander Popov and Andrei Bulatov. However, the first thing that comes to mind is the authenticity of the amateur film and whether it had been edited or tampered with. This could have been easily established through a verification process that included checking for splices throughout, indicating editing of the film. This is exactly what the authors of this article have done.

Alexander Popov and Andrei Bulatov:

> The vast majority of both amateur films and NASA's recordings available on the Internet show the ascent of the Saturn V compiled and edited from separate clips, assembled from individual sequences.[19]

What makes this particular amateur film interesting is that it was filmed continuously for 175 seconds during the launch of Apollo 11 to the first stage separation of the Saturn V and its F-1 engines. That makes this film an excellent source for comparisons to the official film footage provided by NASA to the media.

The amateur film analyzed by Popov and Bulatov was originally filmed by Phil Pollacia on the morning of the Apollo 11 launch. As you will see in Pollacia's background below, he was a very credible witness:

> Phil has a Bachelor's degree from Louisiana Tech University and a Master's degree from Auburn University, both in mathematics. He worked at IBM for NASA. He had the opportunity to become a controller during the Gemini 7/5 – the first rendezvous, Gemini 8 – the first emergency re-entry and Apollo 13. After Gemini, he became the IBM lead manager for Apollo, Skylab and Apollo/Soyuz. Phil himself shot the film on a Super 8 film camera. The shooting and playback speed has not been changed. The Apollo launch footage is one continuous shot without cuts and with no editing. Phil is now 71 years old.[20]

As for Phil Pollacia's motivation in filming the launch of Apollo 11:

> According to Phil's account, the company sent him on a special trip to observe the launch of Apollo 11. He shot the film on a Super 8 camera. His commentaries of the launch are the words of admiration and his sincere belief in this historic event – the missions to the Moon. Associated with long-term work for NASA and honestly convinced in the reality of missions to the Moon, Phil obviously had neither incentive nor motivation to shoot revelatory material. He simply filmed what he saw. This fact makes his material even more unprejudiced and more valuable in exposing NASA's account which has come to light following analysis of his film.[21]

During launch, Apollo 11 cleared the tower in 9.5 seconds. As part of the verification process of the film, other films of the same launch were checked to see if the Apollo 11 launch matched the time clearance of the tower as in the film footage provided by NASA. All of them did, including Pollacia's film.

On the morning of the launch of Apollo 11 the sky was described as being a whitish translucent haze of high cirrostratus clouds. According to Pollacia's film, Apollo 11 passed through the high cirrostratus clouds at 105 seconds.

High cirrostratus clouds are approximately 26,000 feet in altitude. The problem is that at 105 seconds, Apollo 11 should have been at 79,000 feet, not 26,000 feet as is shown on Pollacia's film footage. That means that there were either multiple failures of the F-1 engines or the F-1 engines were not even used. Either way, Apollo 11 could not have reached optimal orbit for translunar insertion, which means there was no landing on the lunar surface.

In fact, at this velocity and height, it's unlikely that Apollo 11 even made it to LEO.

> "With such a start to the flight, the Apollo 11 craft had no chance of catching up with the required ascent schedule", states the veteran of Baikonur Cosmodrome N. V. Lebedev. Indeed, according to NASA's records, the burn of the first stage of the Saturn V is about 60% of 162 seconds. Respectively, by the 106th second the first stage has burnt about 60% of its fuel, and it has made less than 1/8th of its required journey.[22]

After studying the film footage, the authors state that at the 105th second into the launch, Apollo 11 was "three times behind NASA's actual ascent record" and at 107-109 seconds, "the rocket travelled nine times slower than it should have done, according to the NASA record."

Therefore, based on their results, Apollo 11 had no working spacecraft and therefore no astronauts onboard. It also did not have the power to reach LEO and instead ended up in the Atlantic Ocean once out of range of the media.

S. G. Pokrovsky, Ph.D. Comes To Similar Conclusions With The Official Apollo 11 Film Footage

S. G. Pokrovsky conducted a frame-by-frame analysis of the official Apollo 11 launch film footage. In his thirty-five-page article, he too determined that the Saturn V first stage separation happened at a lower altitude than what had been stated by NASA. This fact further indicates that there was no payload for a manned lunar landing.

> In the first approximation with a velocity deficit of about 1150-1200 m/s, it was not possible to put a

deficit of 17 000-18 000 kg into lunar orbit. NASA stated that the mission placed about 46 tons into lunar orbit – 28 tons of which had to be the Apollo craft itself. Since all our speed estimates are upper-bound, the booster payload deficit may have been even higher.

Given these obtained estimates, all arguments over what could have been achieved during the Apollo program should take into account that not more than 28 tons, including the Apollo 11 craft itself, out of 46 tons (as stated by NASA) could have been placed into lunar orbit.[23]

Pokrovsky comes to a slightly different conclusion by stating that Apollo 11 reached LEO, but as with the other scientists in this section, his overall conclusion is that Apollo 11 did not have the necessary hardware onboard for a lunar landing. However, if you factor in his liberal speed "upper-bound" estimates of the Saturn V performance, then by inference, it is the same conclusion as other scientists and that is, Apollo 11 had no crew and never reached LEO and instead, went into the Atlantic Ocean once out of camera range.

The western scientific community has since tried to counter S. G. Pokrovsky's work with the book, *'Moon Hoax: Debunked! Finally, a no-nonsense, fact-filled rebuttal of "moon hoax" claims, for doubters and enthusiast alike'* by Paolo Attivissimo. It's a book that should be read, as it is important to read both sides of this discussion.

Note: You can read Paolo Attivissimo's counter argument regarding the Saturn V's performance in his book or on www.aulis.com.

But the exact facts surrounding the performance of the Saturn V can never be determined, since most of the "fact-filled" documents have disappeared.

Minimal Testing Of The Saturn IB And Saturn V

As stated, Apollo 4 was the first mission involving the Saturn V and was also the first mission to supposedly have used the cluster of five F-1 engines. There was only one more mission, Apollo 6, which involved the F-1 engines but this mission was plagued with problems. We now know that subsequent missions involving the Saturn V either used reduced power in the F-1 engines due to instability of the combustion chamber, or instead, used different engines with less power and thrust. Either way, the Saturn V lacked the power necessary for launching the Apollo hardware into LEO for a manned lunar landing. We will now look at the minimal testing of the Saturn V with its F-1 engines, in the actual conditions of spaceflight.

The Saturn IB and Saturn V were very different when it came to factors like lift capabilities on launch, the effect of atmospheric forces and the trajectory to LEO and beyond. Hence, both the Saturn IB and Saturn V cannot be combined in total spaceflight experience, since their characteristics are different. Further, it was the Saturn V which contained the F-1 engines needed to launch the Apollo hardware into LEO for a manned lunar landing. This makes the overall minimal testing of each these two Saturn rockets in actual spaceflight, especially that of the Saturn V, all the more startling, as is shown below:

- Most of the previous missions leading up to the first manned mission involved different components of the Saturn rocket series, not the complete structure of the Saturn IB or Saturn V itself.
- The 20th mission was the first launch of an actual Saturn IB and the 23rd mission was the first launch of an actual Saturn V.
- Both of these missions were unmanned.

- There were only five unmanned missions of the Saturn IB in the actual conditions of spaceflight, before the first manned mission of that vehicle, with Apollo 7 to LEO.
- There were only two unmanned missions of the Saturn V, with a combined total duration of 19 hours, before the first manned mission of that vehicle.

But when you look further into the testing of the Saturn V, the first stage with its five F-1 engines had only a combined total of approximately four minutes in the actual conditions of spaceflight, before the first manned mission of the Saturn V with Apollo 8. This is very surprising, since we were led to believe that Apollo 8 circumnavigated the Moon and was apparently a flawless mission.

The MSFC had built scale models of both the F-1 engines and the first stage of the Saturn V for wind tunnel testing, which were used for simulating launch, by decreasing atmospheric pressure from approximately 20 to 37 miles in altitude. Aviation used the same method but this was always followed by many hours of testing in actual flight conditions and, as we've seen, NASA in no way matched that level of spaceflight testing. This becomes quite obvious when you compare NASA's testing of the F-1 engines in actual flight conditions, which amounts to mere minutes, to the testing of each new aircraft in actual flight conditions, which amounts to hundreds of hours.

Given NASA's purported proficiency in automation, with numerous unmanned and automated missions to LEO and beyond, including two unmanned missions of the Saturn V, Apollo 8 should have been another unmanned and automated mission, especially given that it was the first Apollo mission to leave LEO to circumnavigate the Moon. This should have been followed by further automated and unmanned missions using the Saturn V to circumnavigate the Moon, in order to accumulate as much data as possible. Data from these Saturn V unmanned missions could have then been studied meticulously, making design modifications where necessary, before sending the first manned mission outside of LEO, therefore increasing the chances of success, like we have been led to believe happened with Apollo 8. This would have been a logical first step.

NASA then could have launched a series of unmanned and automated Saturn Vs, complete with the necessary hardware for lunar landings, again, to accumulate as much data as possible. These data from automated lunar landings could have been studied, making any design modifications necessary, increasing the success for the first manned lunar landing, as we were led to believe happened with Apollo 11. This would have been a logical second step.

Although there had been unmanned landing missions on the lunar surface by both the Americans and the Soviets at that time, it's important to note that, up to the Apollo 11 mission, there was nothing of the magnitude of an Apollo 11 landing. It would have made sense to have numerous unmanned and automated landings with the LM on the lunar surface, aside from computer simulations and the use of the Lunar Landing Research Vehicle (LLRV) and the Lunar Landing Training Vehicle (LLTV) used by astronauts as part of their training to simulate lunar landings. (There will be an in-depth discussion of this in Part 2 of this series). Software simulations were limited with 1960s technology, but as NASA claims, they had access to the AGC on the Apollo missions from Mission Control. So, they could have easily practiced unmanned lunar landing procedures using the Apollo LM in the actual conditions of spaceflight, before the first manned landing.

In addition, there were only four unmanned missions of the CM and five unmanned missions of the SM in the actual conditions of spaceflight before the first manned mission of

Apollo 7. The SM would have been a vital aspect of the Apollo missions, given that it was responsible for providing life support systems and propulsion. NASA had two vacuum chambers, which simulated the vacuum of space, large enough to test the CM and SM. But that doesn't compare to the actual conditions of spaceflight in LEO and beyond. Apollo 8, along with being the first manned mission to use the Saturn V with its cluster of five F-1 engines, was only the second manned mission of the CM and SM.

Further, Apollos 9 and 10 don't amount to much in the way of combined experience for Apollo 11 either. One could argue that the manned Mercury and Gemini space programs should be added in terms of experience, along with Apollos, 7, 8, 9 and 10, which would amount to approximately 2,000 hours of experience in the actual conditions of space leading up to Apollo 11. But that experience should only be applied to astronauts in terms of the human experience in space, since it didn't involve the same design and configuration of the Apollo spacecraft, nor did any of the Mercury and Gemini manned missions involve going beyond LEO. For the Apollo missions, it is the actual missions involving the Saturn V that were paramount. The Saturn V, CM, SM, and LM were more complex in their design, supposedly incorporating new and innovative fly-by-wire technology. Although fly-by-wire technology was already in use in military aircraft at that time, the Apollo missions were the first to use an integrated fly-by-wire computer system. (There will be an in-depth discussion on this technology in Chapter 3).

Therefore, when it came to the testing of new technologies, the same standards used in aviation should have been applied to manned space missions, but obviously this was not the case. In addition to NASA using scale models of the F-1 engines and the Saturn V, they were also running computer simulations at a time when software necessary to run computer simulations was limited. And unlike aviation, which had decades of experience behind it, NASA's manned spaceflight missions to LEO had only a few years of experience and manned missions beyond LEO were non-existent.

To recap, Apollos 4 and 6 were the first two automated unmanned missions of the Saturn V. While Apollo 4 apparently performed as expected, Apollo 6 was plagued with F-1 engines problems which were resolved in just seven months leading up to the next launch of the Saturn V, with Apollo 8.

Apollo 8 was the first manned mission of the Saturn V and the first manned mission to have left LEO to circumnavigate the Moon, and Apollo 10 was the second manned mission in a Saturn V to do the same. Soon after, Apollo 11 became the first manned landing on the lunar surface.

Firstly, NASA's claim that all problems with the Saturn V were resolved in just seven months, before the first successful manned mission of the Saturn V, is questionable. Secondly, NASA's claim of landing the first manned mission soon thereafter on the lunar surface with Apollo 11, really stretches their credibility.

However, the exact facts surrounding the performance of the Saturn V can never be determined, since many of the "fact-filled" documents are incomplete, missing, and/or destroyed (more on this in chapter 6).

Summary

In this chapter we've learned that, for decades, the Soviet Union was first in many of the accomplishments in the unmanned and manned space program, except of course for one brief period when NASA caught up and excelled in their manned space program and landed manned missions on the

Moon, according to the official narrative. After these 'historic' Apollo Moon landings, the Soviets continued for the next couple of decades being, once again, number one in their space program.

The history of the Saturn rocket program goes back to WWII and the German rocket program with Wernher von Braun. There have been some serious allegations made towards von Braun regarding his possible war crimes against humanity. That does not discredit von Braun's purported brilliance in rocket technology. But to recruit a man such as von Braun, it does establish a sense of hubris between these two nations with the goal of being superior in space, rather than the exploration of space for the betterment of humankind.

After analyzing the Apollo series of launches, in particular, the Saturn IB and Saturn V, we've established the minimal amount of testing in actual conditions of Earth's atmospheric forces on launch, as well as spaceflight in LEO. Further, the unmanned launches of the Saturn V itself had only a combined total of 19 hours in actual conditions of spaceflight, before the first manned mission using that vehicle.

Former Rocketdyne employee Bill Kaysing wrote the first book, published in 1976, exposing the Apollo Moon hoax. Through his employment with Rocketdyne, he had access to documents detailing the real power output of the Saturn Vs' F-1 engines. In his book, Kaysing wrote that the F-1 engines did not have the power to launch the Apollo hardware payload into LEO, therefore establishing that no Moon landings took place.

Recently, engineer Gennady Ivchenkov made an in-depth analysis of the F-1 engine and concluded that the combustion chamber was unstable and couldn't have maintained the required thrust to launch the Apollo hardware payload into LEO, substantiating Bill Kaysing's claims from over forty years ago.

Alexander Popov and Andrei Bulatov studied an amateur film by Phil Pollacia, who at that time worked at IBM for NASA. After authenticating Pollacia's film and matching it to the official film provided by NASA and the media, it was determined that Apollo 11 was underpowered for a launch to LEO, negating a manned lunar landing. They further established that Apollo 11 had no crew and the Saturn V more than likely ended up in the Atlantic Ocean.

S. G. Pokrovsky studied the official film footage of Apollo 11 and came to similar conclusions; that this mission was underpowered and could not have launched the hardware payload necessary for a manned lunar landing.

Furthermore, the documents and schematics for the Saturn V have been "lost or destroyed," which is now an established fact.

All of this culminates in the weak performance of the F-1 engines of the Saturn V. The minimum static tests of the F-1 engines were conducted under very controlled conditions, a very different environment from actual spaceflight. However, as we've established, the first stage, with its F-1 engines of the Saturn V, had only four minutes of testing in actual conditions of spaceflight before the first manned mission using the Saturn V, with Apollo 8.

The issue is whether or not the F-1 engines were used in the Saturn V, given that they could not be used at their full power potential. As has been established, the F-1 engines were used for the first time in Apollo 6. But, given the serious problems experienced with that mission, it seems Apollo 6 was the first and last Saturn V to use the F-1 engines, and if they were used at all, they were not used at their full power potential, negating any manned lunar landing.

Given NASA's flight test schedule of approximately twenty-five missions over seven years, leading up to the first manned mission of the Saturn V, a more realistic timetable for attempting a manned lunar landing mission would have been several decades in the future, after many more unmanned and automated missions of the Saturn V. However, since NASA has pushed back an actual manned lunar landing decade after decade since the last faked Moon landing in 1972, we can now foresee several more decades into the future from this present time of 2018.

But a first step for a manned lunar mission requires a spacecraft capable of launch to LEO. As of right now, NASA no longer has that capability.

A combined total of four minutes of the F1 engines in actual spaceflight conditions, before the first manned mission of a Saturn V, is proof enough for an unsuspecting public that NASA had no intentions of sending astronauts anywhere beyond LEO.

Chapter 2 – Endnotes

[1] Jonathan Allday, Apollo In Perspective Spaceflight Then And Now, p. 155.

[2] Dwanye A. Day, 'Thunder in a bottle: the non-use of the mighty F-1 Engine, published March 27, 2006 on www.thespacereview.com

[3] Ibid.

[4] Anthony Young, The SATURN V F-1 ENGINE Powering Apollo into History, p. 203.

[5] Ibid., p. 203.

[6] Ibid., p. 204-205.

[7] Ibid., p. 209.

[8] Jeff Foust, 'Review: The Saturn V F-1 Engine', article www.thespacereview.com

[9] Bill Kaysing, We Never Went To The Moon, p. 62.

[10] Gennady Ivchenkov, 'Evaluation of F-1 characteristics, based on the analysis of heat transfer and strength of the tubular cooling jacket', article www.aulis.com

[11] Ibid.

[12] Op Cit., Young, p. 84.

[13] Ibid., p. 85.

[14] Op Cit., Ivchenkov.

[15] Eugen Reichl, Project Apollo The Moon Landings, 1968-1972, p. 17.

[16] Op Cit., Ivchenkov.

[17] Eugen Reichl, SATURN V AMERICA'S ROCKET TO THE MOON, p. 39.

[18] Op Cit., Ivchenkov.

[19] Alexander Popov Ph.D and Andrei Bulatov, 'Did this Saturn V Rocket Get to the Moon?' www.aulis.com

[20] Ibid.

[21] Ibid.

[22] Ibid

[23] S.G. Pokrovsky Ph.D, 'Investigation into the Saturn V velocity and its ability to place the stated payload into lunar orbit', article. www.aulis.com

Chapter Three

Navigation And The Apollo Guidance Computer

Has Anyone Seen Earth?

The Apollo missions' method of navigation was what piqued my interest and motivated me to begin my research.

It was a method based on celestial navigation that has been used by ships sailing across the oceans for hundreds of years. It is one thing sailing around the world using this method with established geographical land marks and maps, but quite another when you consider the vast distance relative to our technology when making a 480,000-mile round trip in cislunar space. Even with 1960s technology such as the much-touted Apollo Guidance Computer (AGC) which was a fly-by-wire system incorporated into this method of celestial navigation, you'll learn how challenging it would have been to even try navigating in LEO, let alone a 480,000-mile round trip in cislunar space.

The relatively new (for that time) fly-by-wire technology used in the Apollo missions, had been in use in military aircraft since the 1950s. But the fly-by-wire AGC was the first fully integrated system used on any manned mission, let alone, in LEO and beyond. I've pared down the description of this technology in the next two sections for a better understanding.

Fly-By-Wire

Today fly-by-wire technology has become common in the airline industry. In aircraft, fly-by-wire technology has eliminated the need for hydraulics to move control surfaces like the rudder, elevator, and ailerons. For example, in previous aviation technology, the pilot would make inputs on the control column to activate the hydraulics which would move or deflect the ailerons on the outside of the wings to bank the aircraft. This technology has now been replaced in new aircraft like Airbus and Boeing. So, when the pilot makes inputs on the control column, he or she is commanding the computer to send a signal to an actuator to bank the aircraft, replacing the need for hydraulics. Since there are no hydraulics, this method should ideally save on weight and fuel costs, although given today's greed among oil companies, those savings are usually nil.

The first fully integrated use of a fly-by-wire system, with no mechanical or hydraulic backup system, was the Apollo Lunar Landing Research Vehicle (LLRV) which was first flown in 1964 and was used for training the Apollo astronauts. The LLRV was configured to simulate the LM in $1/6^{th}$ gravity for lunar landing practice. This technology was then incorporated into the Apollo spacecraft design. The LM's fly-by-wire system was tested for the first time in actual conditions in LEO with Apollo 9 in March of 1969. The second test of the fly-by-wire system in actual conditions was with Apollo 10 in lunar orbit, with a descent to within 50,000 feet of the lunar surface in May, 1969. Both of these missions were supposed to have been a test run for Apollo 11. Any and all anomalies with the fly-by-wire AGC managed to be sorted out in just four months with only two Apollo missions in the actual conditions of spaceflight.

The first civilian aircraft to use the fly-by-wire technology was the Concorde in 1969 which entered commercial service in 1976. The manufacturers of Concorde decided to err on the side of caution and tested their aircraft's fly-by-wire system for six years before allowing any passengers onboard.

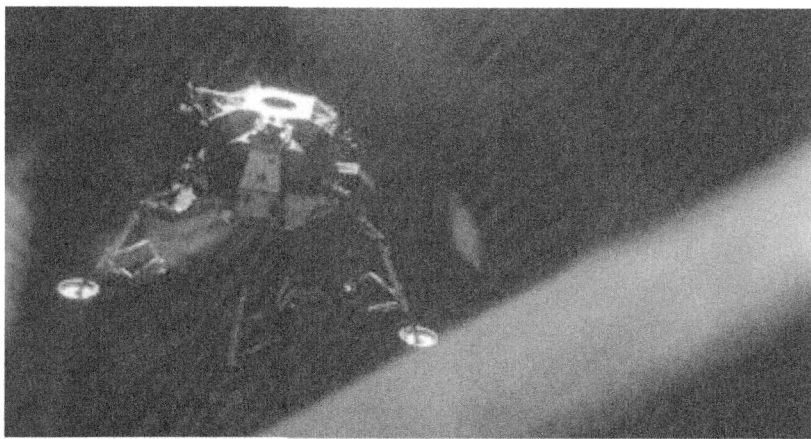

Figure 3.1 – Apollo 10 LM. This photo was taken from inside the CM while in lunar orbit. This was supposedly the second manned flight of the LM in actual spaceflight conditions
Source: NASA

Figure 3.2 – The Concorde
Source - Wikipedia

Apollo Guidance Computer

The AGC was designed by the Massachusetts Institute of Technology (MIT) and manufactured by Raytheon. Each Apollo mission had two of these computers; one for the CM and the other for the LM. The AGC evolved from navigating the CM to the Moon and back to a fully integrated fly-by-wire computer system responsible for attitude, the Reaction Control System (RCS) thrusters for trajectory, and the Service propulsion engine of the CM. The AGC had three main components:

1. The inertial measurement unit (IMU)
2. The optics containing the sextant and scan telescope
3. A computer to integrate the systems including the Guidance, Navigation and Control (GN and C) system.

1. The Inertial Measurement Unit

The inertial measurement unit (IMU) was responsible for detecting the inertial motion of the spacecraft. It consisted of three swiveling gimbals which contained spinning gyroscopes to hold them in place as the spacecraft's position and orientation changed. The principle is the same as the gyros installed in aircraft flight instruments, especially in general aviation although this is now being replaced with the new glass cockpit technology, much like the airlines have been doing for the last couple of decades. For example, the attitude indicator in an aircraft is a gyro instrument with an artificial horizon as a reference for the pilot. The attitude indicator remains fixed in relation to the ground with the aircraft moving around the instrument, therefore giving the pilot pitch, bank and roll information. With the Apollo spacecraft this inertial space was in reference to the stars and given that the Apollo astronauts were military pilots, they requested that a similar instrument be installed in the CM and LM. This was called the Flight Director/Attitude Indicator (FDAI) displaying pitch, yaw and roll angles with the instrument displaying Earth or Moon's horizon to give the astronauts a better sense of orientation.

Figure 3.3 – Flight Director/Attitude Indicator for CM. A similar instrument was used in the LM
Source - NASA

2. The Optics

As part of the navigation system, the Apollo spacecraft had a version of the sextant, called the optics, which was used by sailors for hundreds of years to measure angles between the Earth's horizon, the Sun, and the stars. It consisted of a sextant and telescope. The former was an optical instrument capable of measuring angles between two stars. The lens had a 1.6-degree true field of view with 28x magnification and two lines of sight used for star sightings; one fixed, called the landmark line of sight (LLOS) and one movable, called the star line of sight (SLOS). The SLOS swung up to 57 degrees from the fixed line of sight and was used to bring the star sightings into alignment with the Earth's horizon. Usually, two-star sightings would be sought out and the coordinates fed into the AGC. The telescope part of the optics had a 1x magnification with a 60-degree true field of view.

Since the optics was fixed in position, the AGC would be commanded to position the CSM for star sightings. The Command Module Pilot (CMP) would then aim the telescope at a star and line it up with the sextant. Among programs stored in the memory core of the AGC was a list of angles for 37 bright stars more easily visible to the astronauts. After the CSM was positioned, a program was selected for aligning the IMU. The CMP would then press a switch for the computer to read the angles between stars sightings taken by the optics. This would display the angles on the 'display and keyboard' DSKY (to be explained below) and then used to realign the IMU. From this information, the CMP would obtain the state vector and determine whether a course correction was necessary. This procedure for checking the state vector was done several times on Apollo 11 on the way to the Moon and back.

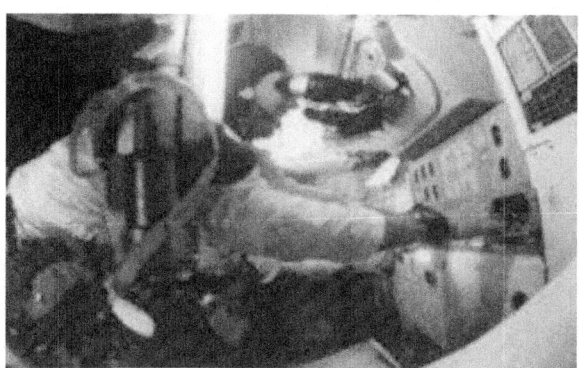

Figure 3.4 – Jim Lovell in the CM of Apollo 8 using the scanning telescope
Source - NASA

3. **Guidance, Navigation And Control System**

NASA wanted this new computer to have autopilot as well as guidance and navigation capabilities, so the computer further evolved into the Guidance, Navigation and Control System (GN and C), commonly referred to as the AGC. Raytheon had to pare down the usual floor-to-ceiling computers of the 1960s to one the size of a cubic foot (approximately) for the CM and LM. This supposedly was accomplished in just one year. The AGC did not store information on a disk. It was stored in read only memory (ROM), which was a core rope memory system. This was accomplished in the manufacturing phase by weaving copper wire through or around a tiny magnetic core. The crew interfaced with the AGC using a digital display and keypad known as the DSKY, pronounced 'diss-key' onboard both the CM and LM. Mission control at Houston also had a DSKY to interface with the AGC for remote control, if and when necessary. Software for the AGC was written in binary assembly or machine language. The 'Interpreter' was used to translate mathematical functions and the 'Executive' managed the programs.

NASA claims that the AGC was capable of running several programs at the same time. And though NASA claims the AGC had autopilot, it did not have autonomous capabilities for finding solutions to the many scenarios that could have endangered the Apollo missions and of course the astronauts.

Figure 3.5 – Apollo Guidance computer and DSKY
Source - Wikipedia

Trajectory And Docking Using The Non-Autonomous AGC

One of the many important procedures for the Apollo spacecraft in maintaining a programmed route to the Moon, was to fire the engine of the S-IVB for a limited time for Translunar Insertion (TLI). This is done to put the spacecraft on a proper trajectory to the Moon. If engine thrust was precise, it would have put the CSM on its proper trajectory, that is, an elliptical orbit around the Earth extending to the far side of the Moon. This is the free return trajectory, which would have put the Apollo spacecraft on a course around the Moon and back to Earth, in the case of a Service Module engine failure. It's interesting to note that subsequent Apollo missions gave up the free return trajectory for the hybrid trajectory. This was apparently done to save fuel putting them on a trajectory to their respective Moon landing locations. NASA considered the risk of a SM engine failure to be minimal, therefore they gave up the free return trajectory. That would have been an enormous gamble to take in a manned mission with one engine, 240,000 miles from Earth.

Proponents of these missions have argued that the LM descent engine could have been used as a backup. However, the LM engine wasn't as powerful as the CSM engine. And given the flimsy design of the LM, it's quite conceivable that structural damage could have taken place during the Saturn V launch, due to atmospheric forces. There are any number of scenarios that could have seriously damaged the LM, therefore relying on that as a back-up would have required, its own back-up. We'll discuss more on the flimsy design of the LM in Chapter 5.

After the S-IVB fired its engine to put Apollo 11 on its trajectory towards the Moon, it was followed by a separation by the CSM which would have had to use its RCS thrusters to move away from the S-IVB. The CSM would then have to turn 180 degrees and move toward the S-IVB to dock with the LM to extract it. The CSM, now docked with the LM, would then have needed to turn 180 degrees back to its original position for its continued trajectory towards the Moon initiated by the S-IVB. Complicated maneuvers like this were supposedly done by a non-autonomous computer.

The Astronauts Would Have Been Marooned In Space

Apollo 11 CMP Michael Collins claims that the Apollo method of navigation had an accuracy of .01 degrees.

Author Ralph Rene writes:
> Collins says he was thrilled when the unit flipped up its five balls in praise, but this represented .01 degree accuracy – not an exceptional result by today's standards. There are 60 nautical miles to a degree and .01 degree equals .6-nautical miles. Many navigators on small wave-tossed boats equal this performance.[1]

Works well in small boats and planes. But on a 480,000-mile round trip?

Ralph Rene continues on with an in-depth explanation in his book using an analogy. I'll use a variation of that analogy to show how easily a spacecraft moving through the vacuum of space can, for a variety of reasons, move off course.

There's a method general aviation pilots use to check their track, called the 1 in 60 rule. This means when you've travelled 60 nautical miles, and are one degree off course, you are now one nautical mile off course. It's an easy situation for pilots to correct on long cross-country trips especially with map readings and references to ground terrain along with navigation equipment, that is, if you correct your track promptly. But with the Apollo missions we're not talking about a cross country trip. We're talking about a 480,000-mile round trip in cislunar space, with little or no tracking capabilities with only the stars as a visual reference, using a non-autonomous computer.

Now apply a version of the 1 in 60 rule to these factors:

- The speed of the CSM while decreasing due to Earth's gravity until the equigravisphere (the gravitational neutral point and where the Moon begins to exert its gravitational influence due to the Apollo spacecraft's track) but still fast by comparison to aircraft.

- The Moon in its orbit moving at a speed of 2,300 miles an hour, which travelled about 155,000 miles in its orbit around Earth as it moved into position for the planned interception by the Apollo spacecraft.

- The celestial method of navigation using a non-autonomous computer that required interface by the astronauts for specific programs. Also, the lack of visual references, that is, the limited options in star sightings available for navigating.

- Having no radio navigation equipment comparable in technology and precision in navigating as aircraft have.

- Having little or no tracking capabilities of the Apollo spacecraft from Mission Control.

These points require an autonomous computer for complex calculations. The AGC did not have this capability, so with the above points factored together, the Apollo spacecraft would have moved off course by thousands of miles for any number of reasons, requiring a delta-v (change in velocity and direction), that needed to use propellant to fire the engine for putting them back on course. And because of weight restrictions for getting into orbit, propellant was limited so there wasn't much, if any, margin for error.

The method of navigation used by the Apollo missions was to check to make sure that they were on course, not to maintain it. The AGC didn't have this capability, which is why checking for any necessary course corrections was done in the first place. This is one of the many scenarios for the limited performance that the AGC would have had to deal with. If this method of navigation were used in actual conditions, this would have been a sure shot recipe for disaster, marooning the Apollo mission astronauts in orbit in cislunar space for eternity.

Tracking Apollo Missions, The NASA Way

Now that we've established that the AGC was not capable of maintaining course, how did the astronauts know when to make course corrections? The answer is they didn't. NASA had to come up with a method for tracking the Apollo spacecraft so they could inform them when to perform a course correction.

Aircraft tracking and navigation is accomplished with ground and onboard equipment. But on spacecraft there are limits to how much weight can be launched. Therefore, everything possible is done to keep it to a minimum. For the Apollo missions, a way had to be determined to track the spacecraft, since radar had a limited range and this needed to be done without bulky equipment and excess weight.

The method NASA came up with was called the Doppler effect. This was supposedly done by Mission control in Houston, Texas. The Doppler effect is usually likened to the horn of an oncoming car which appears to rise in pitch as it's moving towards the observer and then appears to decline in pitch as it moves away from the observer. The actual pitch of the horn never changes. The same method is applied to radio frequencies from the Apollo spacecraft when moving away or towards Earth's tracking stations. However, because of the thermal extremes of space and the excessive equipment needed onboard a spacecraft to send signals of sufficient strength using this method, NASA says it found a way to use the Doppler effect without the need for this excessive equipment on the CM.

> Given that a powerful, accurate radio signal would in any case be sent to the spacecraft to carry voice and data from mission control, engineers simply arranged that it be modified on board in a known way, and re-transmitted back to the ground, this time carrying voice and data from the spacecraft. If the frequency of the signal from Earth was precisely known, then so was the spacecraft------if it were not moving. [2]

After equipment on the ground received the downlink from the spacecraft, the precise frequency was compared to the uplink. A lower frequency meant that a spacecraft was moving away from a ground station, and a higher frequency meant that the spacecraft was moving towards a ground station. NASA claims that this modified method could determine the CM's distance to an accuracy of about 30 meters, which avoided the need for excessive onboard equipment.

The Doppler effect method:
- so precise that it could have been used to track the CM and allow Mission control at Houston to radio the astronauts to make a course correction if needed?

- based on tiny Doppler shifts in radio frequency?
- that determined the CM's position to an accuracy of about 30 meters, anywhere on a 480,000-mile round trip in cislunar space?
- without the necessary equipment onboard the CM?
- relying on no disruption in radio frequency?

Radio and communication failures happen all the time even with today's more sophisticated network. However, since radar wouldn't have had the range needed to track spacecraft in cislunar space back then, NASA had to come up with a method of tracking the Apollo spacecraft, a way that would at least convince the public.

Yet NASA has said that this method worked perfectly for all of the nine Apollo missions that supposedly went beyond LEO. And if it seems NASA was stretching its navigation technique a little, the Apollo 13 incident was another story altogether, which you'll see in the next section.

Theatrics At Its Best

On April 13, 1970, Apollo 13 had an oxygen tank explosion in the Service Module while docked with the LM enroute to the Moon. Although technically, it was an electrical fire that caused an over-pressurization and rupture in oxygen tank No 2 which damaged oxygen tank No 1. However, the over-pressurization was enough to blow the side panel off the Service Module (SM). In the astronauts' 'heroic' attempt to save their spacecraft, they abandoned their Moon landing and powered down the CM to save power, which they would need for reentry into the Earth's atmosphere. Since the CM was powered down, that meant the AGC was powered down as well, which meant no navigation system. They had to rely instead, on the LM's navigation system to get them back to Earth. But because the LM's primary guidance and navigation system (PGNS) would have used too much power, which was now limited, they instead used the back-up computer, the LM's Abort Guidance System (AGS), to help navigate back to Earth.

Meanwhile, the 'explosion' in the Apollo 13 SM was now venting particles which was complicating their ability to distinguish between them and the star sightings needed for position fixes and course corrections. So now, the astronauts are in a serious life-threatening situation in which they have to resort to using a non-autonomous back-up computer with even less power and memory than that of the AGC. And while there were contingencies that included using the LM descent engine in the case of a CSM engine failure, apparently none of them included the Apollo 13 scenario. There's a possible reason for this:

> At the time of the 'Apollo 13' 'accident' on April 13/14, 1970 this Fra Mauro site was actually a considerable distance into the unlit side of the terminator. This is such a crucial point that we sought verification on this circumstance from Dr. Percy Seymour, astrophysicist and Principal Lecturer in Astronomy at the University of Plymouth. England. Percy confirmed that this was in fact the case and kindly supplied us with his own computer printout

illustrating the position of the terminator at 23:30 hours GMT on April 13 1970.[3]

Apollo 13 was inadvertently scheduled to land on the unlit side of the terminator in an area called Fra Mauro. All of the missions were scheduled to land on the sunlit side of the terminator since their only lighting was the Sun. This has been confirmed by other authors using computer software called Celestia, a 3D astronomy program created by Chris Laurel. Somehow, NASA miscalculated the landing of this fictitious mission, so they needed to come up with a solution. Therefore, the Apollo 13 accident scenario was invented to rescue NASA from embarrassment. They obviously made a blunder in planning this mission that would have landed in the dark.

Proponents have countered that Apollo 13 would have landed near the Moon's terminator on the sunlit side. However, given the close proximity to the unlit side and the fact that the astronauts were using visual landmarks searching for a suitable landing site, their approach left no margin for error. This would have been hazardous, to say the least.

Charts And Slide Rules

The Apollo mission method was to use the AGC along with charts and slide rules. Mission Control in Houston would send information by voice to the astronauts for mid-course corrections, not digital data. This required communications and data uplinks to be 100% reliable. There is the probability factor, which usually gives a high percentage of success and reliability, but there are usually back-up systems to increase that reliability. With the Apollo missions' method of navigation, there was no back-up system. This contradicts the safety factor for a manned mission on a 480,000-mile round trip in cislunar space.

A realistic manned mission in cislunar space would require an onboard autonomous computer with the necessary speed and memory capacity for any scenario encountered on a 480,000-mile round trip. That would require programming into the onboard computer's software memory a reference frame for navigating, which was supposedly done. But as has been established, the AGC required crew interface, which would have been time consuming and inaccurate, to say the least.

Realistically, the AGC would have needed an autonomous capability for solutions including constant updates by the nanosecond of the Earth and Moon's orbiting position in relation to the Sun, stars, and most importantly the CM. And note, this would have to have been in real-time. The AGC would then use this data to update projected propellant requirements, velocity, and estimated time enroute to numerous checkpoints on a continuous basis very much like what is done in aviation. As soon as a course correction is necessary, an autonomous computer instantly finds solutions, performs the maneuver, while alerting the astronauts through digital displays. The AGC did not have this capability.

The Limited Capacity And Memory Of The AGC

As mentioned earlier, the AGC required crew interface for altering, updating or switching to another program. For added safety, the main computers at Houston would have been running the same programs for comparison. In fact, NASA claims that the mainframe computers at Houston did the most complicated or biggest part of the computations which were then uplinked to the onboard AGC. That alone raises some serious questions as to the efficacy of the AGC and the safety of any manned mission in LEO or beyond, using this limited technology.

It has been said that the AGC had less computing power and memory than that of the average pocket calculator. This is true considering the AGC had a memory capacity of 38,000 words which is a fraction of any modern personal computer. Proponents of the Apollo missions counter this by saying that unlike today's computers, the AGC didn't have the need for running numerous other programs like displaying video. However, the average modern-day computer isn't responsible for the lives of manned missions outside of LEO in cislunar space on a 480,000-mile round trip.

The information that was uploaded to the AGC, or voiced up for the astronauts to write down, relied on the uplink and communications being 100% reliable. But even with the uplink it still doesn't consider the need for a computer to find instant solutions to any emergencies in cislunar space, e.g.:

(a) an environmental systems failure or
(b) averting possible celestial debris, where even a second's delay could spell catastrophe for the crew.

In a perfect world where absolutely nothing could go wrong, maybe the AGC might have been able to barely complete its task, theoretically that is, and possibly in LEO and even that's a stretch given its purported limited memory as claimed by NASA.

Computer Engineer Xavier Pascal writes:

> Some say that it was not important if the Apollo Guidance Computer was underpowered because it was the mainframe computers back on Earth that were calculating the trajectory of the Command and Service Module (CSM). It is totally impossible for these computers to calculate in advance the entirety of the trajectory commands to the engines, because commands to an engine are only approximate and there is always a slight margin of error – over time such errors accumulate and become significant.[4]

The delay in sending commands from the mainframe computers in Houston to the onboard AGC is about 1.25 seconds and the same time for that signal to come back. That's a total of 2.5 seconds which may not seem like much but in fact is quite long in the case of an emergency. There would have been a further time delay for Houston's mainframe computers, in finding solutions to a specific problem since data was sent up by voice communications which now translates into minutes. An emergency can spell the end of a mission in seconds. You don't have minutes waiting around for Mission Control back on Earth trying to figure out a solution.

Xavier Pascal made comparisons of the AGC to the Univac computer of the same era:

Although the core rope memories of the two computers display similarities, they work in a very different manner, the wires passing through or bypassing the cores being sense wires in the case of the Apollo memory – these wires being activation wires instead in the memory of Univac; in the case of the Univac memory, each core had a unique sense wire, so there was no problem regarding the division of current in the sense wires as with the memory of Apollo. And that fact makes the whole difference between a core rope memory which can work, and one which cannot.[5]

In fact, Pascal's conclusion regarding the AGC is startling:

> In short, this computer had no memory, none at all. Neither ROM nor RAM.
>
> With a DSKY unit which was not working correctly, the AGC definitely appears to be a complete fake. But if this Apollo Guidance Computer was a joke it was because the engineers intended it to be so, and not because they were incompetent. The engineers placed incoherence absolutely everywhere. All the electronic interfaces were stuffed with intentional errors.[6]

The AGC's performance can be summarized as follows:

- Low computing power
- No memory
- Non-autonomous
- A complete fake

Where Exactly Is The Equigravisphere

There's one more curious anomaly and that is regarding the equigravisphere (the point at which Earth and Moon exert an equal pull of gravity also called the gravitational neutral point) which was necessary for the calculated neutral point (CNP) at the date and time of Apollo 11.

After TLI, the Apollo spacecraft would have needed to be precise in reaching the CNP while factoring in its corresponding decrease in forward velocity due to the pull of Earth's gravity. At the CNP, Apollo 11 would then enter the influence of the Moon's gravity therefore increasing forward velocity. So, the pre-calculated time in mission planning becomes vitally important since any discrepancy would require the use of propellant, which was limited due to weight restrictions for launch.

Isaac Newton calculated the average equigravisphere at 215,000 miles from the Earth and 23,900 miles from the Moon for a total distance of 238,900 miles.

Discrepancies in the CNP for the date and time of Apollo 11 are as follows:

- The *TIME* magazine issue of July 1969 listed the CNP as 43,495 miles from the Moon.

- In 1981, David Baker's *Space technology* lists the total distance to the Moon as 253,475 miles. He did not publish the CNP. But his total distance between the

Earth and Moon differs from that of Isaac Newton (David Baker was involved in the Apollo 13 mission).

- *'Space Travel: A History: An Update of History of Rocketry and Space Travel,'* by *Wernher Von Braun, Fredrick I.III Orday and Fred Durant*, lists the CNP as 43,495 miles from the Moon. This corresponds to the *TIME* magazine figures.

- *'Spaceflight and Technology A Chronology'* by *David Baker* published in 1996 puts the CNP at 38,925 miles from the Moon and 214,550 miles from the Earth for a total distance of 253,475 miles. This total distance corresponds to his 1981 publication, but this time, he has published the CNP.

- *The First Men On The Moon - The Story of Apollo 11* by *David M. Harland* puts the CNP at 33,822 nautical miles from the Moon and 186,437 nautical miles from the Earth for a total distance of 220,259 nautical miles.

When these figures are converted from nautical miles to statue miles, David Baker's and David M. Harland's numbers come close. But there's still a discrepancy of several miles. For a manned mission to safely travel to and from the Moon, with limited propellant onboard, precise calculations are imperative.

> Simply put, there cannot be more than one distance between the Earth and Moon on the same date and time; and there should only be one figure for the distance from a given planetary body at which the calculated neutral point (CNP) occurs.[7]

Aside from the obvious propellant required to compensate for any errors in calculations for the CNP, how would they have even known that they had reached the CNP sooner or later than expected? The AGC would not have had the capability for detecting this. Therefore, given the discrepancies in the figures above, this is another scenario in which the astronauts could have found themselves marooned for eternity in cislunar space.

NASA has never explained this discrepancy.

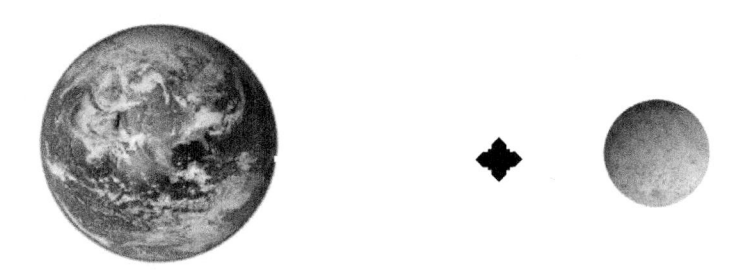

Figure 3.6 – The Earth & Moon gravitational neutral point
Illustration - Author

Redundancy – Hand And Eye Coordination

As for redundancy in the case of an AGC failure, and unlike Apollo 13 without the LM and its onboard PGNS or AGS on its route back to Earth, NASA says the Command Module had a second control system that could operate independent of the other systems, called the stabilization and control system (SCS).

> This stabilization and control system (SCS) could maintain attitude and allow the crew to make accurate maneuvers and, if necessary, even manually control the SPS engine.[8]

In other words, NASA says that if necessary the astronauts could have hand flown the CSM 240,000 miles back to Earth with nothing more than hand and eye coordination.

Summary

Fly-by-wire technology had been used in military aircraft for a decade before the Apollo missions. But the Apollo missions were the first to use a fully integrated fly-by-wire computer system and that was in LEO and cislunar space, an unpredictable environment in which little or nothing was known.

The AGC had no capacity or memory to run the programs necessary to circumnavigate the Moon, and it lacked an autonomous capability for any contingency or emergency that could have been encountered anywhere in cislunar space.

Further, Apollo 13 could not have navigated safely back to Earth given its circumstances, along with using a computer system in the LM with even less power and memory of the AGC.

Visual references, charts and slide rules, were necessary components of their method of navigating along with the

AGC. But as computer engineer Xavier Pascal concluded, the AGC was a "complete fake."

The numerous scenarios that would have been encountered, would have marooned the Apollo astronauts in an elliptical orbit around the Earth for an eternity.

NASA had no way to track the Apollo missions anywhere along the 480,000-mile round trip, so they modified a method based on a variation of the Doppler effect.

There seems to be discrepancies regarding the Earth and Moon gravitational neutral point during Apollo 11, which would have thrown all the calculations for their track into disarray, leading to more course corrections, which would have depleted their limited sources of propellent. One of many scenarios that would have marooned the Apollo astronauts.

As redundancy, NASA says the Apollo astronauts could have hand flown the CM 240,000 miles back to Earth.

So here you have a non-autonomous computer that NASA says worked perfectly for all 11 Apollo missions, including nine beyond LEO, six of which supposedly landed on the lunar surface and all seemingly with perfection. But proponents argue that these missions were not perfect and use the fictional account of the Apollo 13 near disaster and the small anomalies with the other missions often cited, as examples, that the AGC could handle any contingency.

In aviation, it is often said a good or perfect landing is one in which you walk away from. With the Apollo missions, all of the astronauts made it back to Earth, none worse for the wear. In fact, the Apollo missions were not only perfect, they were a little, too perfect.

W. David Woods writes:

> There is poetic beauty to the Apollo flights which lies in the fact that the crews navigated between worlds by sighting the very stars their ancestors would have employed to guide boats and ships across the oceans of Earth.[9]

The Apollo 11 mission is said to have successfully completed its 480,000-mile round trip in cislunar space with the following:

- A non-autonomous computer
- Low computing power
- No memory capacity
- Using charts and slide rules
- With manual control as redundancy

W. David Woods calls this navigation method, "poetic beauty."

> On the contrary, it's called, "pure insanity."

Chapter 3 - Endnotes

1. Ralph Renee, NASA Mooned America, p. 63.

2. W. David Woods, How Apollo Flew To The Moon, p. 158.

3. Mary Bennett and David S. Percy, Dark Moon Apollo And The Whistle-Blowers, p. 349.

4. Xavier Pascal, Article - 'Was the Apollo Computer Flawed?' www.aulis.com

5. Ibid.

6. Ibid.

7. Op Cit., Bennett, Percy, p. 393.

8. Op Cit., Woods, p. 179.

9. Ibid., p. 151.

Chapter Four

Radiation Belts Around The Earth, Intense Solar Storms & Galactic Cosmic Rays

To glow, or not to glow!

The Apollo missions would have had to travel through an area of radiation surrounding the Earth called the Van Allen belts. This is an area of intense radiation and there has been much discussion over the years regarding NASA's claim that, given the right shielding and trajectory, the Apollo missions were able to travel through the radiation belts with little or no harm to the astronauts. However, when one actually goes through the literature regarding the Van Allen belts, conflicting pieces of information become apparent. Today NASA admits that there are many problems that need to be solved before sending manned missions through the Van Allen belts, which will be discussed in detail in this chapter.

However, the subject of background radiation on Earth and in space is a very complex one and when it comes to the latter, designing protective shielding for spacecraft isn't as straightforward as is often presented in the media. Then there's the danger of micrometeoroids and thermal control, that needs to be factored into spacecraft shielding design as well.

In this chapter, we'll focus on the dangerous radiation environment, which presents a constant threat to any manned space mission, including the area of space beyond Low Earth Orbit (LEO) and outside of the Earth's magnetic field. Instead of focusing on the actual design of spacecraft shielding, this chapter will delve into an oft-used term in spacecraft shielding, attenuation of radiation.

To completely block radiation in the space environment, the spacecraft requires shielding of different materials, for example lead or enormous amounts of water. Due to the excess weight of these materials, a launch would be near impossible with the technology available today. Therefore, spacecraft shielding is designed to decrease the intensity of radiation to acceptable limits for astronauts using materials that minimize weight for launches. This is what's called attenuation of radiation. It is the claims made by NASA when discussing attenuation of radiation, that we'll focus on. Spacecraft shielding that would actually be needed for radiation in space in LEO and beyond, as well as for protection from micrometeoroids and thermal control, will be discussed in Chapter 5.

Factors to consider in the attenuation of radiation and accumulated dosages include:
- the overall health of astronauts
- gender and age
- number of previous manned missions they may have been on
- the duration of any specific manned mission they may be considered for. For example, a particular astronaut's previous mission(s) depending on the duration and

exposure to radiation, may disqualify him or her for any future mission.

It would take many books to talk about the history and theory of radiation and its effects on people, more specifically astronauts in the space environment. However, for most of us, myself included, a brief review of some of the basics on this subject will help in appreciating the complexity involved, which I've provided in the next section.

Basic Theory

There are three sources of radiation in space:

1. High energy particles around the Earth trapped by the magnetosphere called the Van Allen Belts.
2. Solar storms which originate from the Sun which are referred to in several ways. For example:
   - solar cosmic ray events
   - solar proton events
   - solar energetic particle events
   - energetic storm particle events
   - ground-level events
   - proton showers
   - solar cap absorption events or as is commonly referred to as Solar Particle Events (SPEs).

   Also, there are Coronal Mass Ejections (CMEs), which are associated with SPEs. In this book, we'll refer to the terms SPEs and CMEs.
3. Galactic Cosmic Rays (GCRs) which come from the Sun and from all directions outside the solar system.

Guidelines most commonly used for reference are from the International Commission on Radiological Protection (ICRP) and the International Commission on Radiation Units and Measurements (ICRU). Basic measurement units are used as a reference point in an effort to appreciate and understand some of the challenges for spacecraft shielding and the attenuation of radiation. For more detailed information, you can refer to the ICRP and ICRU.

There are four aspects of radiation to consider:

A) Absorbed Dose

There are two types of radiation; ionizing and non-ionizing. Examples of Ionizing radiation include, alpha particles, beta particles, x-rays and gamma rays, all of which are harmful and measured as an absorbed dose by the unit, joule per kilogram (J/kg). In physics, 1 J/kg is called a gray (Gy). Outside of the Earth's atmosphere, astronauts need protection from ionizing radiation in LEO and beyond. This becomes even more important for astronauts as they venture beyond LEO and the Earth's protective magnetic field.

B) Equivalent Dose

Since there are different types of radiation, there needs to be a further method of determining its biological effects. Proponents of the Apollo missions say that alpha radiation in the outer regions of the Van Allen belts can easily be stopped with a few centimeters of air or paper, while beta radiation can be stopped with aluminum, thus giving the impression that a manned mission through this region would cause little or no harm to the astronauts, as long as they travelled through this area quickly. This is partially correct. However, as this chapter will show, NASA is not sure of the energy levels in this region of space around the Earth and if alpha particles are inhaled or ingested, they can be the most destructive form of ionizing radiation.

Given that alpha and beta radiation will have different biological effects, a numerical Quality factor (Q) between 1 and 20 is used to determine the equivalent dose. Alpha particles are given a Q factor of 20, since it causes more harmful biological effects once ingested. Beta and gamma radiation are assigned a Q factor of 1. Alpha and beta are forms of particle radiation that are relatively easy to stop. Even though gamma radiation is assigned the lowest Q factor, it can be the most penetrating causing enormous harm to astronauts, depending on its energy.

Therefore, 1 Gy of alpha radiation is 20 times more harmful than 1 Gy of beta or gamma radiation. The Sievert (Sv), which is the international unit system (SI), is used to interpret the varying biological effects from different types of radiation.

For reference purposes:

- 1 Gy of alpha radiation is an equivalent dose of 20 Sv.
- 1 Gy of beta radiation is an equivalent dose of 1 Sv.
- 1 Gy of gamma radiation is an equivalent dose of 1 Sv.

Other types of radiation are given different Q factors between 1 and 20.

C) Effective Dose

Since different types of radiation can strike different parts of the body, a new quantity called the effective dose is used in which each organ or part of the body is assigned its own Q factor. This is one of many factors considered when designing spacecraft shielding.

The figures used above in equivalent dose, are further broken down into millisieverts (mSv), so 1 Sv is equal to 1000 mSv. It is mSv that is usually used in determining the effective dose for individuals.

And when using figures such as 0.01 mSv or 1 Sv, you still use the (Q) factors 1 to 20 to multiply them.

D) Dose Rate

A dosimeter is used to measure the dose rate, usually in mSv per hour. The Apollo astronauts were supposed to have carried a dosimeter onboard. Although <u>average</u> dose rates for the Apollo astronauts have been released, <u>individual</u> dose rates remain classified.

The Rad And The Rem

The absorbed dose was referred to as the rad, while the equivalent dose was referred to as the rem. Thus, these are old terms used which have now been replaced by the Gy and Sv.

The average yearly dose per person in background and man-made radiation in the United States is approximately 0.62 rems which is 620 mrems, or as expressed in the new unit, 0.0062 Sv, or 6.2 mSv.

Many of the science and engineering books I've referred to have used the old units of rems. I'll refer to this term and use 0.62 rems as the approximate average per person yearly dose in the United States, as a reference point, when discussing attenuation of radiation and how many rems astronauts could have been exposed to. There are many online conversion tables that can be used to convert rems to sieverts if necessary.

I hope this brief description will help in your research into the Apollo Moon missions when reading about shielding and the attenuation of radiation, which will be discussed below.

Van Allen Radiation Belts

The Van Allen radiation belts are two regions of energetic particles that encircle the Earth, excluding the north and south polar regions. Any manned mission to the Moon would have required a trajectory through the radiation belts which NASA claims is safe for astronauts, as long as they have proper shielding as they travel through outer regions of the outer radiation belt quickly, therefore minimizing radiation exposure.

Discovery Of The Van Allen Belts

In 1958 Dr. James Van Allen discovered two radiation belts surrounding the Earth through two unmanned missions:
- Explorer 1 (launched February 1, 1958) and
- Explorer 3 (launched March 26 1958).

The inner and outer radiation belts consist of energetic charged particles, the inner belt consisting predominately of protons and the outer belt of electrons.

Dr. James Van Allen writes:
> The inner belt reaches its peak at about 2,000 miles from the Earth, the outer one at about 10,000 miles. Beyond 10,000 miles the radiation intensity diminishes steadily: it disappears almost completely beyond 40,000 miles. The maximum intensity of radiation in each belt is about 25,000 counts per second, equivalent to some 40,000 particles per square centimeter per second.[1]

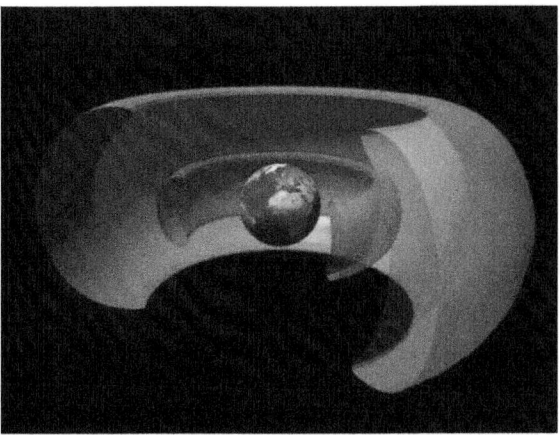

Figure 4.1 – The Van Allen Belts
Source: Wikipedia

Solar wind is tenuous ionized gas called plasma and is the main source of energetic charged particles in the radiation belts. The solar wind or ionized gas encounters the Earth's magnetic field by first hitting the magnetosheath which is often referred to as the bow shock. This area extends approximately 37,000 miles from Earth. Below the magnetosheath is the magnetopause, and below that is the magnetosphere. From here, these charged particles in the magnetosphere, mainly protons and electrons, are trapped inside Earth's magnetic field. Within Earth's magnetic field, these charged particles are now influenced by Earth's magnetic north and south poles, travelling along magnetic field lines. Hence the Van Allen belts are in constant flux and form one of many pertinent factors to consider when sending manned missions through this area.

Figure 4.2 – The Solar Wind from the Sun hits the Bow Shock and is deflected around Earth's magnetic field
Source: Flickr & NASA

Conflicting Information Regarding Intensity Of The Van Allen Belts

People who question the Apollo missions are usually referred to as conspiracy theorists. This term was invented by the CIA to dispel any rumors of conspiracy regarding the JFK assassination. Further, 'conspiracy theorists' are often accused of 'quote mining.' It's another term used in an attempt to further discredit anyone writing about this subject. Quotes are used by authors all the time and I will use them in this chapter to show the discrepancies and conflicting information regarding the Van Allen belts. We'll start with conflicting information regarding the size and energy levels of the radiation belts as is presented in numerous books and articles.

Here are several points taken from six sources that show the discrepancies and conflicting information regarding the Van Allen belts. After each source, I offer my analysis:

1. Dark Moon Apollo And the Whistle-Blowers by Marry Bennett & David S Percy:

    - In *Spaceflight and Rocketry: A Chronology* David Baker has an entry dated March 20 1959 for an announcement of further radiation belt data from Professor James Van Allen, stating that the inner belt extended from 1,500 to 3,000 miles, the upper belt from 8,000 to 55,000 miles.

    - Yet the same year, in the highly respected *Scientific American* James Van Allen stated that the radiation zone extends to 64,000 miles.

    - In 1997 NASA web sites quoted the starting point of the Van Allen Belts at between 250-

750 miles from Earth. Hardly a start point, more of a vague zone!

- Also, in 1997 British university students were also informed that the Van Allen Belts extend from 621 to 3,107 miles for the lower belt and that the upper belt only continues to a mere 12,430 miles!

- The above distance is even more astonishing with the upper belt apparently ending 51,570 miles short of Van Allen's own data.

As this list compiled by Bennett and Percy shows, there are several different interpretations of the data. It would provide some clarification if the scientific community could at least agree on where the radiation belts start and where they finish, considering the solar wind that extends the Earth's magnetic field on the side away from the Sun. In any manned space mission, an absence of precise data as to the extent of the radiation belts means that an exact length of time which is safe for astronauts to be exposed to radiation, can't be determined.

2. Radiation and The International Space Station Recommendations to Reduce Risk, by Space Studies Board, Board on Atmospheric Sciences and Climate, National Research Council:

- One component of the belts, the outer-belt MeV electrons, has long been known to be highly variable. Fluxes frequently vary by several orders of magnitude, with an interval of

> high flux observed typically once a month. Though MeV electrons rarely penetrate into the interior of spacecraft, they can be hazardous to astronauts performing EVAs.
>
> - Most of the other components of the belts, including highly penetrating energetic protons, are generally much more stable and predictable. However, we now know that that stability is not absolute.

The actual data for the outer electron flux, is not defined in their text. Does this mean there's a possibility that these several orders of magnitude of MeV electrons have the potential of penetrating a spacecraft's shielding posing a serious risk to astronauts? Yes, it does and their quote "MeV electrons rarely penetrate into the interior of spacecraft" means they can penetrate given the magnitude of the flux.

The information from the second source above, is a contradiction in terms, and is particularly significant, as will be seen next.

> 3. Space Radiation Hazards and the Vision for Space Exploration, Report of a Workshop by National Research Council Of The National Academies:
>
> - The region of trapped radiation within Earth's magnetosphere consists of energetic protons, electrons, and heavy ions organized in two belts, a relatively stable proton-dominated inner belt and a highly variable electron-

> dominated outer belt. Energies range from approximately 100 keV to greater than 400 MeV for protons and from 10s of keV to greater than 10 MeV for electrons. Manned missions in geospace are flown in low Earth orbit at altitudes below the inner belt; however, astronauts embarking on or returning from journeys to the Moon or Mars will have to pass through the Van Allen belts and will be exposed for brief periods of high levels of radiation.

We just learned from the National Research Council's previous quote from source 2, that the inner proton belt stability "<u>is not absolute</u>." Yet, in the quote just above from source 3, they're now saying, that the inner proton belt is "relatively stable," therefore insinuating that it's <u>now absolute.</u> This is a major contradiction.

It would also help to know what the intensity of these "high levels of radiation" are, as they were to have been determined during the Apollo missions 50 years ago. But decades later, they are now questioning radiation intensity in this region. So, either NASA has lost this data, or they never had it to begin with.

4. How Apollo Flew To The Moon by W. David Woods:

- For a few minutes, as they raced away at 10 kilometers per second, the crew passed through the van Allen belts, where they received a small dose of radiation. There is an inner torus populated by energetic protons, which the spacecraft passed through in a matter of minutes, and against which the spacecraft's skin was an effective shield. The spacecraft took about an hour and a half to traverse the more extensive outer torus, but this region has mainly low-energy electrons and so was less of a worry to mission planners.

Notice how W. David Woods quickly skims over the issue of attenuation of radiation with his phrase, "the spacecraft's skin was an effective shield." This quote also represents more conflicting information regarding how long each Apollo mission would have taken to travel through the Van Allen belts.

As to how long the Apollo missions were in the radiation belts, depends on the source, as I have read several estimates, none of which seem to agree. The graph below shows different estimates by various groups as to how long the Apollo missions were in these regions of the Van Allen Belts.

Proponents of the missions	Inner Belt	Outer Belt
David W Woods	Few minutes	1.5 Hours
Group #1	0	1-2 Hours
Group#2	15 minutes	1 Hour

On a matter as important as this, all sources should agree and as is evident, they don't.

5. Dr. James Van Allen in Scientific American, March, 1959:
    - Unless some practical way can be found to shield space-travelers against the effects of the radiation, manned space rockets can best take off through the radiation-free zone over the poles.

This is interesting since the discoverer of the radiation belts, Dr. James Van Allen, has said that manned missions should travel an area through the north or south poles, where there is little or no radiation. Near the end of this chapter, you'll see why it took Dr. Van Allen over 30 years to refute his own statement about manned missions safely travelling through other regions of the Van Allen belts, besides the radiation-free zones.

6. An Introduction To Space Weather by Mark Moldwin:
    - The radiation belts contain intense radiation that can kill astronauts and damage or destroy sensitive electronics on spacecraft. Understanding this region is one of the main efforts of space weather since many important satellites have their orbits in or through the radiation belts.

NASA recently posted a YouTube video with one if its engineers, Kelly Smith, talking about the intensity of the radiation belts and the need to solve numerous problems before sending manned missions through them. Proponents say that the intensity of the radiation belts Kelly Smith talks about only applies to sensitive modern electronics onboard new spacecraft. Mark Moldwin's above quote shows that's partly true, but radiation intense enough to harm sensitive electronics, can also harm or kill the astronauts. Smith completely ignores the Apollo missions' travel through the outer regions of the radiation belts and he doesn't specifically say in the video, where those radiation intensities are. Hence the inference is, it's not safe for manned missions no matter what area of the radiation belts these missions attempt to go through, and that's with 21st century technology.

Reference: View the video on YouTube, by typing in 'NASA engineer admits they can't get past the Van Allen Belts.'

Note: With the exception of Dr. James Van Allen, all the above quotes come from sources decades after the Apollo missions.

There's one more thing to add here and that is the variations in Earth's magnetic field over the South Atlantic. It's an area of the Van Allen belts that dips to an approximate altitude of 100 miles over Brazil and stretches out over the south Atlantic Ocean, commonly referred to as the South Atlantic Anomaly (SAA). Special precautions on board the International Space Station (ISS) need to be taken whenever travelling through this region because of intense proton radiation. On the one hand NASA says all manned missions needed to avoid the intense inner proton radiation belt, while on the other hand, all manned Apollo missions spent 10-15 minutes travelling through this inner belt with no apparent health effects on the astronauts. This represents more conflicting information from NASA.

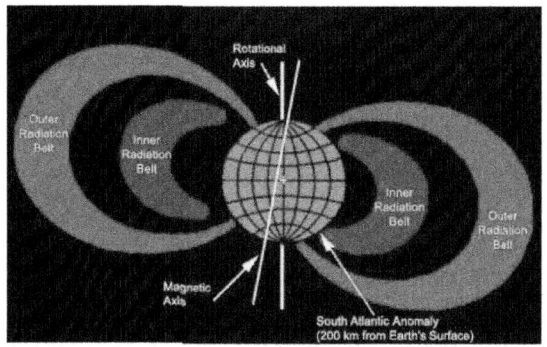

Figure 4.3 – The South Atlantic Anomaly (SAA)
Source: Wikipedia

Outer Electron Belt Would Have Exceeded Apollo Spacecraft Shielding

In this section, we'll use the terms keV, MeV and GeV:
- ➤ keV (kilo-electron-volt which is 1 thousand electron volts).
- ➤ MeV (mega-electron-volt which is 1 million electron volts).
- ➤ GeV (giga-electron-volt which is 1 billion electron volts).

A reference point to remember for the Apollo missions is the attenuation of radiation up to 14.7 MeV electrons in the predominately electron outer Van Allen belt.

Being exposed to "high levels of radiation" for short periods of time is tolerable but of course, you'd want to know what the energy flux of these "high levels of radiation" are. The proton

AP-8 and electron AE-8 Radiation Belt Models of 1976 say that electron energies are no greater than 7 MeV in the outer Van Allen belt. Yet as was mentioned above, the National Research Council published its report in 2006 and said electron energies are greater than 10 MeV.

However, in their 2008 publication the National Research Council refers back to the AP-8 and AE-8 models of 1976:

> The trapped particle models in current use are the AP-8 for protons and the AE-8 for electrons (Sawyer and Vette, 1976). Although the AP-8/AE-8 models are still widely used for spacecraft design, it is recognized that they are severely outdated because of the secular changes in Earth's magnetic field since the era when the measurements underlying the models were made. It is also now recognized that radiation belts vary on timescales shorter than just the solar maximum/solar minimum levels described in the AP-8/AE-8 models (e,g., Blake et al., 1992; Li et al., 1993). NASA's Living with a Star program's Radiation Belt Storm Probes, which are scheduled for launch in 2012, are expected to provide measurements that will be the basis for new models. In the meantime, there are also efforts aimed at extending the capabilities of existing models and improving their accuracy through re-analysis of existing datasets (Ginet and O'Brien, 2007; Ginet et al., 2007). Beta versions of the new models (designated AP-9 and AE-9) are scheduled for release in the 2009 to 2010 time frame. Efforts at improving models of Earth's trapped radiation are important for other

NASA missions, as well as for DoD and for the commercial use of space.[2]

Now we're back to the Van Allen belts with electrons no greater than 7 MeV. So, which is it? 7 MeV electrons, or greater than 10 MeV electrons? Since The National Research Council says there are electrons greater than 10 MeVs, how high do these electron energy fluxes go? This is the most important question of all since NASA claims the Apollo spacecraft shielding can stop electrons, up to 14.7 MeVs, the reference point mentioned above.

The 1976 AP-8/AE-8 Radiation Belt Models have been used by proponents of the Apollo missions in an attempt to prove that the Van Allen belts were safe for manned missions to travel through, using the method NASA claimed.

Decades ago, NASA was confident in its technology to send manned missions through the Van Allen belts. However, it now seems that NASA and scientists in general, are more perplexed about the Van Allen belts than ever before. This is disturbing since spacecraft shielding design is based on the AP-8 and AE-8 models, which now conflicts with the National Research Council's estimates. And with the new AP-9 and AE-9 models, NASA still doesn't know how high the electron energy fluxes are, which is discussed in detail next.

Clash Of The Titans

A well-known Australian researcher by the name of Jarrah White has been questioning the validity of the Apollo missions for years through his excellent videos, which you'll find on his

YouTube channel. He has raised some very interesting but disturbing questions about the Apollo missions that NASA refuses to answer. However, NASA is not without its defenders. One of these defenders is Robert A. Braeunig who got into a very interesting and revealing, albeit indirect, online discussion with Jarrah White.

Braeunig published an online article in which he attempts to counter 'conspiracy theorists' regarding claims that the Van Allen belts are harmful to any manned mission attempting to travel through them, including the outer Van Allen belt.

Note: Braeunig claims to be a Civil Engineer and an average person fascinated by rocketry and space flight. You can search for his article online by typing his name along with the Van Allen belts and you can check out his other work at www.braeunig.us.

Braeunig, in his article, shows the actual supposed trajectory through the outer regions of the outer radiation belt. Using mathematics, he explains that given the right method and spacecraft shielding as is claimed by NASA, the Apollo missions could have safely traveled through the outer regions of the outer belt. His basis for the data is the 1976 AP-8/AE-8 model of the Van Allen belts. When you read through all the mathematics, you realize that he's using estimates to formulate his own theoretical model. There is no real-time data for the Apollo missions in Braeunig's article regarding the regions of the outer Van Allen belt and as we'll soon see, his data conflicts with that of other scientists involved in researching the Van Allen belts.

Jarrah White counters Braeunig's online paper with his own use of mathematics, although it is the source of his data that is most interesting. In his YouTube video 'Radiation Reloaded,' White discusses the data regarding the Van Allen belts, focusing on the trajectory of the Apollo missions. Twenty-four minutes into the video, he specifically counters Braeunig's claims that in White's previous YouTube video, he had used erroneous data to prove that the outer Van Allen belt would have been dangerous for any manned mission.

While Jarrah White was researching for a university assignment, he came upon a credible source. In an article by Herbert O. Funsten and his team from the Los Alamos National Laboratory published on March 8, 2013, Funsten talks about penetrating radiation saying electron fluxes are typically observed at energies greater than 15 MeV in both radiation belts, with inner belt proton energies that can exceed 100 MeV. According to the published reports by the National Research Council in the years 2000-2008, energies greater than 30 MeV protons can penetrate the mid-deck of the Space Shuttle. Hence, one should assume that the Apollo spacecraft would be no different. This is interesting considering NASA's claims that the Apollo spacecraft shielding was enough to stop up to 14.7 MeV electrons.

White contacted Funsten and asked him to "quantify the fluxes of the electrons." Funsten referred White to one of the other authors of the article, a space physicist, Dr. Geoffrey D. Reeves. In his correspondence with White, Reeves, a world expert on the subject, made a startling statement. I've reproduced it here in its entirety from Jarrah White's YouTube video 'Radiation Reloaded' to avoid misrepresentation:

Dr. Geoffrey D. Reeves:

The answer is, we don't know.

Most places in the magnetosphere there are essentially no electrons with energies greater than 1 MeV. They just don't stick around long enough. In the inner magnetosphere they can be trapped for a long time. Trapping in the inner belt is much longer than trapping in the outer belt so the fluxes greater than 10 MeV electrons tend to be higher and steadier in the inner belt. How high? How steady? I'm not sure.

Here's why.

1) You need a really large detector to measure greater than 15 MeV electrons. Large means heavy so we typically don't fly detectors that massive. The measurements we do have are typically inferred from backgrounds in detectors that are intended for other purposes and for which the electron response sensitivity is not well known.
2) Integral measurements like Van Allen's Geiger tubes can tell you the total counting vote of electrons that trigger a response in the detector but the sensitivity as a function of energy is not well known. It's an integral measurement but at some point, the sensitivity falls off. For instance, when an electron passes all the way

through a detector it will only deposit part of its energy.
3) Bremsstrahlung. Any material around the detector will produce x-rays when hit by very energetic electrons. Those x-rays will often also be measured by the detector. But now the collecting area you assume isn't the entrance to the detector it's the whole spacecraft.

It is for all these reasons that AE-8 only goes to 7 MeV. You will have to either extrapolate the spectrum and integrate it numerically or you will have to dig into the original literature and look into both the measurements and the caveats.

I'm sorry I can't just give you "the answer". For the purposes of our study (designing a detector that properly measures greater than 50 keV and ions in a region where greater than 15 MeV electrons are present) it was sufficient to know that they can be a problem. We didn't need to know the exact fluxes.

The Van Allen Probes satellites have an instrument called REPT that may provide the measurements we need but it's still going to take a lot of work to extract the correct values given the problems I outlined above.

Cheers
Geoff

Dr. Geoffrey Reeves specifically says that the reason the 1976 AE-8 radiation belt model goes to 7 MeV is because they didn't have the capability to detect anything higher. This confirms that NASA had no way of knowing the electron energy fluxes of the area of the Van Allen belt traversed by the Apollo missions and as Reeves also points out, "it's still going to take a lot of work to extract the correct values given the problems I outlined above."

Another problem he mentions is bremsstrahlung. As common sense would dictate, if spacecraft shielding is not enough to attenuate radiation to acceptable levels for the astronauts, then it follows that the Apollo astronauts would have been exposed to high levels of radiation. However, on the flip side, too much metal shielding can produce x-rays which are just as harmful to astronauts, therefore also leading to an increase in the radiation count. The only way then to attenuate radiation levels to acceptable limits for the astronauts, would be to have real time data on the radiation belts on a consistent basis and then design spacecraft shielding accordingly, or more realistically, avoid these areas altogether. NASA did not have this real-time capability for collecting data on the radiation belts.

As Jarrah White points out, Braeunig tries to get as much mileage out of the 1976 AP-8/AE-8 Radiation Belt Models as possible. Braeunig goes on to say that 0.1 MeV to 3 MeV electrons represent 99.95% of the outer electron belt along Apollo 11's trajectory and that for all practical purposes, electrons greater than or equal to 6 MeV do not exist. As Braeunig says, according to "credible sources," there are virtually no electrons above 14.7 MeV, which is convenient for his narrative, since the claim is the Apollo shielding can attenuate electrons up to 14.7 MeV.

Who exactly are Braeunig's "credible sources?"

Three, Maybe Four, Radiation Belts

In the 1950s, the United States had launched into space, a series of three nuclear warheads under the code name Operation Argus and detonated them below the Van Allen belts.

- ➤ The first warhead was launched August 27, 1958 to an altitude of 110 miles.

- ➤ The second warhead was launched August 30, 1958 to an altitude of 190 miles.

- ➤ And the third warhead was launched September 6, 1958 to an altitude of 493 miles. Each warhead had a yield of 1.5 kilotons and they were detonated over the South Atlantic Ocean.

The kiloton yield in these warheads may not have been considered significant, yet it was determined that x-rays from these explosions could penetrate spacecraft and disable electronics as well as cause radio noise. To make matters worse, this area includes the SAA, where the more intense inner proton belt dips to an approximate altitude of 100 miles.

It was reported that after the detonation of these warheads, the Earth's ionosphere was temporarily disrupted. There were magnetic storms and disruptions in short wave radio communications, and additional electrons were trapped in the magnetosphere forming an artificial radiation belt comparable to the Van Allen belts in intensity. Sir Bernard Lovell, an English physicist and radio astronomer, was particularly concerned and said, regarding Operation Argus, that the "scientific results were somewhat alarming."

So now there are three radiation belts. NASA doesn't say exactly when this artificial radiation belt dissipated, but confirms that during the manned Mercury missions, it no longer existed. However, it can be inferred that it took at least three years for this radiation belt to disappear. However, by 1961, they were back to two radiation belts.

There was also the launch of Operation Starfish Prime, another nuclear warhead. This was particularly troubling since this time they used a megaton bomb. This detonation was at least 1000 times more powerful than the Argus bombs. It was launched July 8, 1962 and detonated 19 miles from Johnston Island in the Pacific Ocean at an altitude of 248 miles. On August 20, 1962 the Atomic Energy Commission, the Department Of Defense and NASA issued a report stating:

- The Solar cells of several satellites had been damaged.
- Measurements made in Peru calculated that the rate of radiant decay would be slow and 10% of radio noise would still be present in two years' time.
- More than one hundred trillion, trillion electrons from the fission product had been trapped by the Earth's magnetic field which formed a new radiation belt at an

altitude of 2,484 miles, with intensity over a hundred times greater than the naturally existing radiation belts.
- The newly formed radiation belt was 400 miles wide and 4,000 miles deep with a possible half-life of 20 years.

Bennett and Percy write:

> The length of a half-life is of paramount importance, as Professor John Davidson pointed out. Essentially it continuously slows down, which means that the artificially-induced radiation created by Starfish Prime would be dropping to a half of its original quantity by 1982; to a quarter by 2002; to one eight by 2022; and that even by 2042 we would still be at one sixteenth of the original amount of radiation. As the original dose was measured at 100 times in excess of the natural radiation levels, this means that by the end of this millennium this artificial belt still contains a level that is descending from between 50 to 25 times the already intense background levels of that region of the Van Allen belts.[3]

NASA says the artificial radiation belt caused by Operation Argus dissipated by 1961. That gives the impression that there were only two radiation belts during the Mercury missions. But the Mercury missions took place before and after Operation Starfish Prime, so there were actually three radiation belts during the Mercury missions. And although the artificial radiation belt caused by Operation Starfish Prime was at a higher altitude, there would have been no way of knowing the effect of any energy flux for that whole region. Furthermore, it took until 1982 for levels to drop to half its quantity and the

Apollo missions are said to have taken place between 1969 and 1972.

Then in 2012, NASA says it discovered a third radiation belt surrounding the Earth. Shouldn't it be a fourth radiation belt? NASA claims that although this 'third' radiation belt dissipated months later, they can only speculate as to what caused it. The prevailing theory is that this 'third' radiation belt was most likely caused by a solar particle event (SPE).

The question is, if NASA's theory is that a third radiation belt can form during an SPE, then how long would that 'third' radiation belt have been there? One, two, three, or four months? Or, instead of months, is it years? After all, NASA insinuated that it took three years for the artificially formed radiation belt caused by Operation Argus to dissipate. However, as has been established, the artificially formed radiation belt caused by Operation Starfish Prime, is still there.

This means that all of the Apollo missions would have had to travel through three or more radiation belts; the inner Van Allan belt, the outer Van Allen belt, and at least one artificial radiation belt formed by operation Starfish Prime.

As pointed out, by the end of the 20th century, levels of radiation in the artificial belt caused by Operation Starfish Prime would have been "between 50 to 25 times the already intense background levels of that region of the Van Allen belts." When this artificial radiation belt is factored in, all of the astronauts of the Apollo missions would have been exposed longer to extremely high levels of radiation than was reported, preventing any safe passage for manned missions through the Van Allen belts regardless of NASA's claims.

There have been numerous SPEs over the decades, so the exact number of radiation belts has yet to be determined. The graph below summarizes the discrepancies and conflicting information supplied by NASA over the decades.

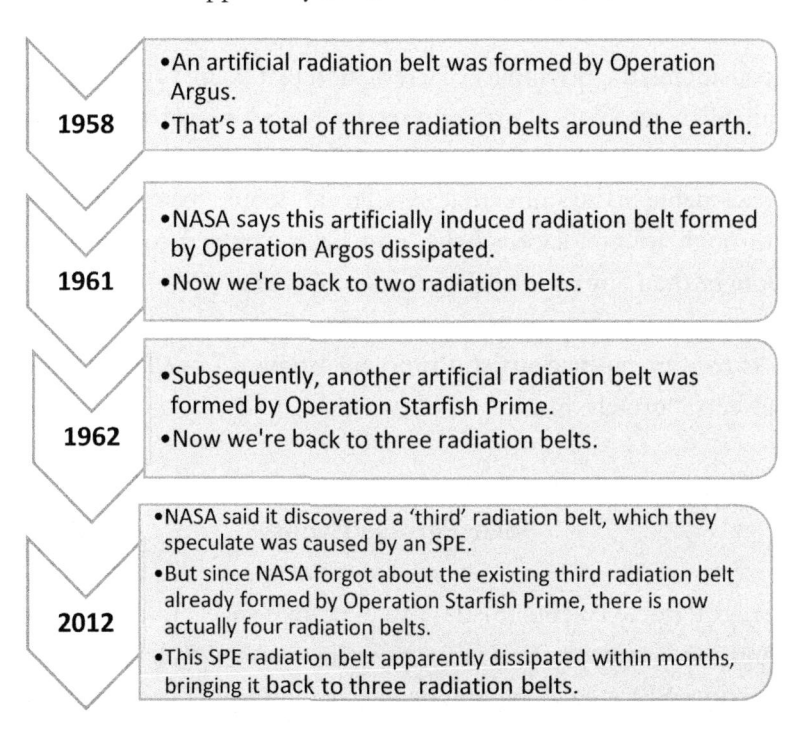

1958
- An artificial radiation belt was formed by Operation Argus.
- That's a total of three radiation belts around the earth.

1961
- NASA says this artificially induced radiation belt formed by Operation Argos dissipated.
- Now we're back to two radiation belts.

1962
- Subsequently, another artificial radiation belt was formed by Operation Starfish Prime.
- Now we're back to three radiation belts.

2012
- NASA said it discovered a 'third' radiation belt, which they speculate was caused by an SPE.
- But since NASA forgot about the existing third radiation belt already formed by Operation Starfish Prime, there is now actually four radiation belts.
- This SPE radiation belt apparently dissipated within months, bringing it back to three radiation belts.

The 2012 discovery of a third radiation belt raises an interesting point. NASA speculates that this third radiation belt was formed by an SPE.

If NASA is right, then it's reasonable to assume that a radiation belt was formed by the SPE event of August 4, 1972, which was four months before the Apollo 17 mission.

Also, what about the intensity of this 'third' radiation belt formed by the August 4, 1972 SPE? It's already been established that electron fluxes are typically observed at energies greater than 15 MeVs, which exceeds the Apollo spacecraft shielding. And how would NASA have even known about the formation of another radiation belt in 1972? There's nothing in the literature back then to suggest that NASA even considered the possibility of a radiation belt being formed from an SPE, which is a proven fact by NASA's own statement, which is discussed at the end of this chapter. However, it is reasonable to assume that Apollo 17 would have travelled through four radiation belts, and been exposed to radiation longer than any of the other Apollo missions.

As for Operation Starfish Prime, Sir Bernard Lovell called the effects, "cataclysmic."

Solar Particle Events

Solar Particle Events (SPEs) can penetrate spacecraft shielding and the best protection is to avoid them. As we'll learn in this section, SPEs have varying degrees of intensity depending on the source. As SPEs are an evolving science, they are and have always been difficult to predict. As with the Van Allen belts, we encounter a subject rife with discrepancies and conflicting information.

SPE Basics

Accelerated SPE particles are surrounded by plasmas and fields and can produce electromagnetic emission from microwaves to gamma rays. They can accelerate electrons up to 10 MeV and protons up to and greater than 100 MeV. As quoted by the National Research Council "Protons comprise 90% of the energetic ions produced in an SPE" and as mentioned, protons above 30 MeVs can penetrate the mid-deck of the space shuttle. This is a very serious situation for any manned mission, to be caught in this solar event.

Given that SPEs can arrive on Earth within minutes, there would be little or no time for any manned mission to prepare for one. As for preparing for an SPE, the only solution would be to seek the relative safety of LEO which would put any manned mission below the Van Allen belts and well within Earth's magnetic field, which would offer some protection. But seeking the protection of Earth's magnetic field, would require getting there quickly from cislunar space. Given the propulsion systems used in spacecraft during the Apollo era and today, 'getting there quickly,' would be an impossible task. Another solution was to turn the CSM around, hoping the Service Module will take the brunt of the SPE, which was supposed to have been one of the procedures for any encounter. Either way, you have a doomed mission.

SPEs are classified as A, B, C, M and X with A being the smallest. Solar flares are often associated with magnetic storms, that is, CMEs. The National Oceanic and Atmospheric Administration (NOAA) further classifies these storms into 3 categories:

- Geomagnetic Storms from G1, G2, G3, G4 and G5

- Solar Radiation Storms from S1, S2, S3, S4 and S5

- Radio Disturbances / Blackouts from R1, R2, R3, R4 and R5

Each category number means, minor, moderate, strong, severe and extreme, respectively.

On January 20, 2005, the National Oceanic Atmospheric Administration (NOAA) issued an advisory for a category S3, a solar radiation storm. This advisory warned that this specific storm had an influx of high energy protons of greater than 100 MeVs. The advisory went on to say that a rare Ground-Level Event (GLE) was observed. GLEs are an increase of ground-level neutrons and are associated with high energy protons greater than 500 MeVs. It seems NASA may be holding back information about the August 4, 1972 SPE.

Maximum SPE Activity During Apollo Missions

Bennett and Percy write:

> The named Apollo astronauts are, however, a remarkable healthy bunch considering that during nine alleged trips to the Moon, 1,506 solar flares were recorded------an average of 16.92 per day per mission. J A McKinnon NOAA expert on solar flares states that 10 to 20% of solar flares could be considered a Medium X-ray emitter event and 1%, the deadliest of all, a Class X event. So, these astronauts should

have encountered from 16 to 33 Class M events and at least one Class X event on each mission.[4]

As NASA admits, the Apollo missions took place during solar maximum when large SPEs were expected to occur. The reason for this is presumably that it fit in with President Kennedy's timeline for manned missions to the Moon by the end of that decade which coincided with the years 1969 to 1972. Therefore, given the timeline set by President Kennedy, it seems NASA had no choice and wrote the script accordingly. As mentioned earlier, there was an SPE on August 4, 1972 whose intensity surprised even NASA. It makes one wonder why NASA would take such a chance of sending a manned mission beyond LEO after this SPE, with minimal shielding and experience with such missions.

> The Apollo missions were scheduled to take place during solar maximum years, when large solar particle events are more apt to occur.[5]

With the quote above, The National Research Council reiterates the point regarding solar maximum. Either it didn't occur to them that the Apollo missions were in potential danger outside of the protective shielding of Earth's magnetic field, or they mentioned it without explanation hoping people would not question the insanity of such a momentous decision sending manned missions beyond LEO.

The National Research Council:

> The problem is serious. Over the past 20 years, radiation effects have caused between one and two satellites per year

> on average to suffer total or partial mission loss. Satellites at low latitudes in low Earth orbit (LEO) stay relatively safe by ducking the intense part of the radiation belts higher up. But at higher altitudes and higher latitudes, where Earth's radiation belts reside and radiation from solar storms invades, radiation hazards cannot be ignored.[6]

The above quote also applies to satellites owned by corporations who don't even bother to report any problems after an SPE, since there's no regulation that says they have to. Hence, the real number of satellites that are affected by solar storms aka SPEs, is obviously higher. There are people who will point out that there are very few interruptions in communications and internet services, inferring that satellites function well regardless of SPEs. However, it should be noted that communications and internet services are primarily facilitated by underground and underwater fiber optic cables.

The National Research Council:

> It delivered a total dose of radiation over half a day that, had it missed the middle and hit the Apollo mission at either end, would have caused the crew in the lunar module to suffer acute radiation sickness and given the uncertainty in the estimate, possibly even death.[7]

This is regarding the SPE of August 4, 1972, four months before Apollo 17. This was the largest solar storm ever recorded in the 20th century. NASA says this storm was about 400 rems yet according to Dr. Percival McCormack, the Manager for Operational Medicine in the Life Sciences

Division of NASA, says it would have delivered 960 rems without shielding.

If the Apollo astronauts were in the LM when this happened, it would have been akin to having little or no shielding and the Command Module wouldn't have been much better. As we've established, approximately 0.6 rems is the yearly average dose per person, so with a dose of 960 rems over a very short period of time, none of the Apollo astronauts would have survived or at the very least, they would have been quite incapacitated. The figure of 960 rems is what is mentioned in NASA reports and given what we've learned so far, this figure is most likely higher as SPEs have known to be in the more energetic GeV range.

Hence, if any of the Apollo missions had been caught in this SPE, their demise would have been instant.

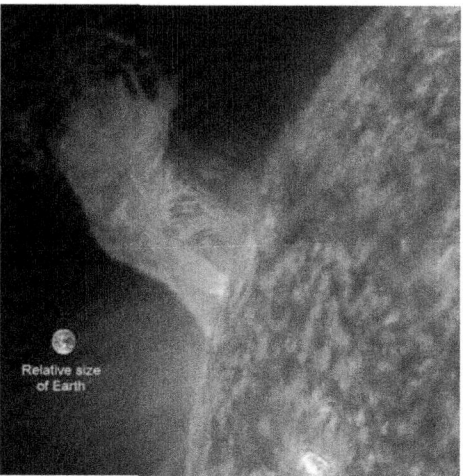

Figure 4.4 – Solar Particle Event. Notice the Earth by comparison
Source: Wikipedia

SPEs Are Unpredictable

SPEs are unpredictable and dangerous to any manned missions outside of LEO and 'experts' can't always explain the mechanisms of SPEs since it is an evolving science, as they themselves admit.

Given the unpredictability of SPEs, it stretches credulity that NASA would even take a chance of sending manned missions to the Moon after the solar event of Aug 4, 1972, which, as previously mentioned, they are supposed to have done with Apollo 17. And that's just one SPE that we've talked about. According to the NOAA, there were 489 SPEs in July of 1969, the same month of the Apollo 11 mission. Also note, in that same year NOAA recorded 7,153 SPEs.

The National Research Council:

> A solar flare and radio burst occurred during the Apollo 12 mission, which had exercised the operational procedures.[8]

The National Research Council had an opportunity to explain what Apollo 12's "operational procedures" were, but failed to do so. In fact, in their three published reports from 2000 to 2008, there is a total of one and a half pages of data from the Apollo missions and at best, that information is scant.

Bennett and Percy write:

> Their mission occupied 14.6% of the overall Apollo profile of 89 days and the average of 268

> solar flares recorded during that time was 17.7% of the total number of flares that actually occurred during the Apollo period. Considering the inability of the agency to clad its craft against lethal radiation------and with figures like these------how long each astronaut actually spent on the surface of the Moon, exposed to lethal radiation, is fairly academic.[9]

This quote is regarding Apollo 15 which experienced the greatest number of SPEs, and apparently the greatest avoidance of them.

More Conflicting Information

NASA says that in the event of an SPE, the shielding on the Apollo spacecraft would have attenuated 400 rems to less than 35 rems and to reiterate, the average yearly dose per person for background and man-made radiation is approximately 0.62 rems. Their contingency for this includes a "quick trip back to Earth" for medical care, which you'll find on NASA's website. Given the level of technology regarding rocket propulsion then and now, the fact that the Moon has no atmosphere and no magnetic field to protect it from SPEs and that it would take three days to get back to Earth, NASA needs to define what a "quick trip back to Earth" is. Proponents of the Apollo missions say that 35 rems is safe for short durations, that is, if you believe the shielding capabilities of the Apollo spacecraft. The National Council on Radiation Protection and Measurements (NRCP) says 35 rems in survivable, but it's obvious (as will be discussed in Chapter 5) that the LM's flimsy design and shielding would not have attenuated 400 rems or 960 rems, to acceptable levels for the safety of the astronauts.

For the most part, Earth's atmosphere and magnetic field protects us from these harmful rays but, outside of the Earth's magnetic field, they are some of the most penetrating forms of radiation and a hazard to any manned mission. During the 1950s, the only way to detect solar particles within SPEs was through ground-based instruments. These particles were secondary particles called muons which had reached the instruments on the ground. But for these particles to reach the instruments on the ground, the solar particles within SPEs had to have exceeded the MeV range with extremely high energies, greater than 4 GeV, to penetrate the Earth's magnetic shield. So, if 30 MeV protons can penetrate the mid-deck of the space shuttle, it doesn't take much to determine what greater than 4 GeV particles can do to astronauts with the level of shielding that the Apollo spacecraft had. A minimum amount of aluminum wouldn't have offered any protection for the Apollo astronauts anywhere outside of LEO.

The conflicting information between the above quotes of 400 rems and 960 rems for the August 4, 1972 SPE, as well as what would have happened to any of the astronauts if they had been caught in this SPE, is disturbing. Given this conflicting information regarding SPEs and NASA's procedural protocols, the reality is that the Apollo astronauts would most likely been vaporized. Proponents sneer when you mention the possibility of astronauts being vaporized by an SPE. However, since SPEs can reach into the GeV range, there is no shielding to protect the astronauts with present technology, so astronauts being vaporized is a real possibility.

It has been rumored that the Soviets had sent several creatures and a cosmonaut to the Moon with their Zond space program in September 1968. When the craft returned and was retrieved from the ocean, the creatures and cosmonaut were rumored to have been vaporized and the American government was notified about this. I haven't been able to substantiate it, so for now, it'll remain just that; a rumor. But the Soviet Zond space program did exist and the official record does show that a mission with small creatures on board was sent to the Moon and back with seemingly little or no harm to the creatures.

> In September 1968 they flew an unmanned Zond round the Moon, and in November of the same year another craft, loaded with tortoises, flies and worms, took the same trip. Then for once, the Russians hesitated. They wanted more tests. The cosmonauts wanted to go, but they were held back. The Americans might still fail------it was better not to risk all so soon.[10]

Figure 4.5 – Soviet Spacecraft – similar to the Zond Spacecraft
Source: Wikipedia

Tortoises can survive thousands of times the radiation than humans. And rather than err on the side of caution (as the

Soviet's did) by sending an unmanned Apollo spacecraft to circumnavigate the Moon, the Americans instead sent the first manned mission, i.e. Apollo 8.

And, it would be interesting to know the real reason the Soviets, "hesitated."

Coronal Mass Ejections

Coronal Mass Ejections (CMEs) are believed to be associated with SPEs and are just as dangerous, though the actual mechanics of this are still not understood.

> Coronal mass ejections consist of large, balloon-shaped clouds of solar plasma and magnetic field that contain up to 10 to the 16th grams of matter and reach speeds in access of 2,500 km/s. The kinetic energy alone is sufficient to boil the North Atlantic Ocean. CMEs are associated with solar flares and solar energetic particle events and occur most often during sunspot maximum. Most of the energy in such events is associated with the CME and not the flare.[11]

One doesn't need to be an expert in space physics to know the consequences of being caught in the middle of a CME, which has enough energy to boil the North Atlantic Ocean. To reiterate, the Apollo missions supposedly took place during solar maximum. Proponents of the Apollo missions are quick to point out that SPEs and CMEs are not omnidirectional, thus insinuating the chances of being hit by one is minimal. It's true that SPEs and CMEs are not omnidirectional, but they are reflected by the Sun's magnetic field, effecting a much wider area in the solar system making any manned mission outside of LEO just as vulnerable no matter what area of the Sun these emissions emanate from. Therefore, this would have increased the chances of an Apollo mission being hit by an SPE and CME. Although CMEs move slower, they can reach Earth in approximately 48 hours, so there wouldn't be a lot of time for any manned mission in cislunar space to seek the relative safety of Earth's magnetic field.

Just like SPEs, the prediction of CMEs is difficult. In the 1960s, NASA had several observatories stationed around the world and as the National Research Council reiterates, prediction of solar storms is difficult, even today. So SPEs and CMEs are a serious risk to any manned mission outside of LEO during solar minimum or maximum years. In other words, prediction of SPEs and CMEs when sending manned missions outside of LEO is far from being an exact science and not something that should be ignored when it comes to the safety of astronauts.

Galactic Cosmic Rays

Now that we've established the hazards of sending manned space missions through the Van Allen belts as well as the dangers of SPEs and CMEs, the Apollo astronauts would have also had to contend with Galactic Cosmic Rays (GCRs).

There are two sources for GCRs:

- radiation that comes from the Sun called solar energetic particles and

- radiation entering our solar system from all directions called <u>galactic cosmic rays</u>.

GCRs contain extremely high energy protons, alpha particles, and heavy nuclei. Cosmic rays are measured in the MeV and GeV range. They represent about a third of the radiation in space.

Figure 4.6 – Command Module and Lunar Module.
The LM had even less protection than the CM
Source: Wikipedia

Although GCRs are always present, cosmic rays from outside the solar system are at a minimum during intense SPE activity from the Sun. As previously mentioned, the Apollo missions took place during that period of intense SPE activity. However, with that intense SPE activity comes solar energetic particles, another form of cosmic rays. Yet, the National Research Council has said that manned missions to Mars will require much more protection in shielding thickness to counter the steady GCR exposure as well SPEs. A manned mission to Mars will take several months compared to a manned mission to the Moon, which would take three to four days. However, there's no reason to assume why the same level of protection in shielding shouldn't be applied to manned missions to the

Moon, especially during extravehicular activities (EVAs) on the lunar surface where astronauts have only their zipped-up spacesuits for protection against GCRs, SPEs, and CMEs.

Mary Bennett and David S. Percy write:

> These might be 'technical terms' used by 'experts', but when presented to the general public there is the potential for the manipulation of reality through vocabulary. The dividing of space into cislunar space (the region of space within the orbit of the Moon) and deep space, (beyond lunar orbit) lulls the public into false assumptions concerning the safety of manned spacecraft and has little to do with the reality of the space environment.[12]

When discussing shielding, NASA tends to use terms like cislunar space and deep space, giving the impression that radiation between the Earth and Moon is more tolerable than between the Moon and Mars, as per the above quote. It's an attempt to differentiate space beyond LEO giving the public the impression that the dangers of radiation in cislunar space is minimal compared to deep-space, that is, in the case of a manned mission to Mars. There's no difference in intensities with SPEs, CMEs, and GCRs between the areas of the Earth, Moon, and Mars. You would require the same level of shielding for any manned mission, regardless of the duration and distance of the mission.

As for dosimeter readings of the astronauts, NASA has supposedly released the average dosages that the astronauts received during the mission, but the actual specific dosimeter readings for each astronaut are classified. It has been 50 years since the first Apollo mission, so why the secrecy about the Apollo astronauts' dosimeter readings that it needed to be classified, especially considering that NASA has supposedly released the combined average dosages the Apollo astronauts received? There can only be two reasons, one is that the readings don't exist, or two, they never went any further than LEO. It's interesting to note that the average Apollo 11 dosimeter readings are comparable to readings on the International Space Station in LEO.

A Quote Here, A Quote There

Anyone who's read any of the numerous books on radiation in general, knows that no two scientists can agree on the effects of radiation on Earth, whether it's natural background radiation or man-made. Yet how interesting it is that the few scientists who have studied NASA's data on the Van Allen Belts, SPEs, CMEs and GCRs, agree on every aspect of them, while other scientists who haven't even bothered to research it for themselves, agree to its validity when reading other scientists' research papers on this. This method of peer reviewed papers, should be approached with caution, given some of the recent disclosures of fraud within the scientific community and the influence of fiduciary obligations.

In the previously mentioned online article, Robert A. Braeunig went out of his was to try and discredit anyone who questions the Apollo missions by labelling them 'conspiracy theorists,' and then went on a rant about their supposed tactics.

Braeunig writes:

> Absent the ability to perform a proper quantitative solution, the conspiracists are forced to look for circumstantial evidence. They can generally do little more than point out what they believe to be suspicious activity or resort to *quote mining*.[13]

Quotes are used all the time by many people on both sides of this discussion including Braeunig himself and there's nothing wrong with it. But there's a reason he specifically mentioned the 'tactic' of *'quote mining,'* since there are some very interesting quotes made by scientists and professionals themselves when specifically talking about the Apollo missions and related subjects, as these statements more than cast doubt on the validity of these missions.

In fact, quotes can actually destroy decades of research. An example of this was recently revealed in the prestigious medical magazine The Journal of the American Medical Association (JAMA) when it disclosed how three Harvard scientists were paid approximately $25,000, fifty years ago to falsify their research on heart disease. For the last five decades, hundreds of thousands of scientists, doctors, and journalists were manipulated into believing a fabricated story. It's disturbing, that very few of these professionals questioned the findings of these three Harvard scientists. What is even more disturbing, is the fact that millions of people around the world who trusted these Harvard scientists were possibly harmed by these 'trusted' professionals. Therefore, thanks to Robert Braeuning, we'll close this chapter by showing the importance of *"quote mining"* by professionals who, inadvertently or on purpose, show how quotes can undo decades of research by challenging established beliefs.

Dr. James Van Allen regarding the radiation belts:

> Our measurements show that the maximum radiation level as of 1958 is equivalent to between 10 and 100 roentgens per hour, depending on the still-undetermined proportion of protons to electrons. Since a human being exposed for two days to even 10 roentgens would have only an even chance of survival, the radiation belts obviously present an obstacle to space flight. Unless some practical way can be found to shield space-travelers against the effects of the radiation, manned space rockets can best take off through the radiation-free zone over the poles.[14]

Ten roentgens is 9.329664 rems and 100 roentgens is 93.296637 rems. As established earlier, the average yearly dose per person for background and man-made radiation in the United States, is approximately 0.62 rems. As Braeunig will quickly point out, Dr. Van Allen mentions a human being exposed for two days, while the Apollo astronauts spent a total of two hours traversing the outer region of the outer radiation belt. However, we've learned that NASA doesn't fully understand the radiation belts and there is evidence of electrons far greater than 15 MeV which exceeds the Apollo shielding capabilities. So, two hours or less in the radiation belts may well have been enough to have seriously harmed the Apollo astronauts, that is, without even considering the artificial radiation belt formed by Operation Starfish Prime.

Further, the Apollo missions apparently spent 15 minutes in the most intense inner dominated proton belt which NASA itself says manned missions must avoid. However, as has been established by Jarrah White, NASA doesn't know for sure the energy flux of these high energy protons and electrons in both the inner and outer radiation belts. So, 15 minutes in the inner dominated proton belt may well have been enough on its own to have seriously harmed the Apollo astronauts, given their lack of shielding.

As I mentioned earlier, it took over 30 years for Dr. Van Allen to refute his own statement about manned space missions traveling through the radiation-free zone around the north and south poles. In response to a one-hour documentary called 'Conspiracy Theory: Did We Land on the Moon?' shown on FOX TV in February 2001, Dr. Van Allen reportedly said this in an *email*:

> However, the outbound and inbound trajectories of the Apollo spacecraft cut through the outer portions of the inner belt and because of their high speed spent only about 15 minutes in traversing the region and less than 2 hours in traversing the much less penetrating radiation in the outer radiation belt. The resulting radiation exposure for the round trip was less than 1% of a fatal dosage - a very minor risk among the far greater other risks of such flights. I made such estimates in the early 1960s and so informed NASA engineers who were planning the Apollo flights. These estimates are still reliable.

So now the Apollo spacecraft spent two hours in the outer electron belt? Again, depends on the source. This data is supposed to have come from NASA, so why is there conflicting information? And as we've seen, "estimates" are anything but reliable. And where is Dr. Van Allen's scientific paper refuting his own work? To say it in an email, doesn't qualify and there are questions as to the source of this email. At any rate, an email refuting a previous scientific paper is not exactly considered part of the scientific realm.

Given what we've established here, Dr. Van Allen's original remarks in his scientific paper in 1959 about manned missions travelling through "the radiation-free zone over the poles" would seem the most logical and safest; that is, going around the radiation belts, not through them.

Barbara B. Poppe:

> The sight of Armstrong walking on the Moon was so unbelievable and amazing that there were those who refused to believe the images they saw and swore the landing was a hoax and a conspiracy.[15]

It's interesting that Poppe, a retired employee of the NOAA actually said this and it makes you wonder why a scientist would even mention the word conspiracy. Is she hinting at something? Quite possibly, as you'll see in her next quote:

> Apollo 11 turned out to be one of a string of lucky Apollo missions that were not hampered by space weather events, which was something of a miracle. Any number of space weather disturbances could have

endangered the lives of the astronauts either directly or by damaging equipment.[16]

Now there's a quote that lacks confidence if not downright skepticism about the validity of the Apollo missions.

As previously mentioned, in 2012 NASA says that it had discovered a third radiation belt. On August 30, 2012, NASA launched the Relativistic Electron Proton Telescope (REPT). A NASA article says that before REPT was activated September 1, 2012, solar activity on the Sun had sent energy to Earth causing the two existing radiation belts to increase in size. According to NASA, it is this energy that caused the formation of a third radiation belt. NASA says that this newly formed belt lasted approximately four weeks.

Here's proof that as recent as 2012, NASA never even considered the possibility of a third radiation belt formed from solar storms:

> Then something happened no one had ever seen before: the particles settled into a new configuration, showing an extra, third belt extending out into space. Within mere days of launch, the Van Allen Probes showed scientists something that would require rewriting textbooks.[17]

This quote from the article on NASA's website throws into question decades of research regarding the Van Allen belts. And it's not a very confident statement coming from a space agency that claims it solved the problem of sending manned missions through the Van Allen belts fifty years ago. It further shows that NASA had no way of knowing if another radiation belt had formed by the August 4, 1972 SPE, four months before Apollo 17. It also appears that NASA hasn't learned much from Operation Argus and Operation Starfish Prime either. As we've established with Operation Starfish Prime, as of 2012, that's four radiation belts, not three.

Kelly Smith, the NASA engineer in the YouTube video previously mentioned, uses terms like "Extreme radiation" and "Dangerous radiation" to describe the Van Allen belts. Further on in the video he says, "We must solve these challenges before we send people through this region of space," when talking about the Orion spacecraft. Apparently, they solved the problems during the Apollo missions but for some reason, these problems need to be solved again.

Given all the facts, the evidence proves that none of the Apollo missions traveled through the Van Allen belts.

Summary

The Apollo level of shielding was inadequate to attenuate radiation to acceptable levels for the safety of the astronauts, given the fact that there is evidence of high energy electrons in the radiation belts that cannot be detected by NASA.

There is conflicting information:

- About how the Apollo missions travelled through the predominately proton inner belt, which is not as stable as NASA thought and would have been a hazard to any manned mission.

- As to the number of artificially and naturally formed radiation belts.
- As to the amount of time the Apollo missions supposedly spent travelling through the outer radiation belt.
- As to the prediction and strength of SPEs and CMEs.

NASA was unable to provide real-time data for the Apollo Moon missions as to the energy flux in the Van Allen belts, instead using a theoretical model based on incomplete data. Further, NASA was caught by surprise by the severity of the August 4, 1972 SPE, yet four months later they supposedly launched Apollo 17, knowing full well that if there was another SPE of this magnitude, the astronauts would not have survived.

GCRs are clearly the most penetrating form of ionizing radiation and since these energies can reach into the GeV range, it is clear Apollo spacecraft had inadequate shielding. In addition, the actual dosimeter readings for each individual astronaut are classified, which is bewildering since NASA has released average accumulated dosages.

Given what I've shown here, *"quote mining,"* as Braeunig calls it, is not only necessary, but vital to the continuing research that will enable future manned missions to eventually travel through the Van Allen belts.

But as NASA said, "that would require rewriting textbooks."

Chapter 4 - Endnotes

[1] Dr. James A Van Allen, Radiation Belts around the Earth, published in Scientific American March, 1959

[2] National Research Council Of The National Academies, Managing Space Radiation Risk in the New Era of Space Exploration, p. 39.

[3] Mary Bennett and David S. Percy, Dark Moon Apollo And The Whistle-Blowers, p. 309.

[4] Ibid., p. 99.

[5] Space Studies Board, Board On Atmospheric Sciences And Climate, National Research Council, Radiation And The International Space Station Recommendations to Reduce Risk, p. 19.

[6] Ibid., p. 7.

[7] Ibid., p. 7.

[8] Ibid., p. 20.

[9] Op Cit., Bennett, Percy, P. 393.

[10] Jonathan Allday, Apollo In Perspective Spaceflight Then And Now, p. 163.

[11] National Research Council Of The National Academies, Space Radiation Hazards and the Vision for Space Exploration, p. 28.

[12] Mary DM Bennett, Orion, the Van Allen Belts & Space Radiation Challenges, www.aulis.com

[13] Robert A. Braeunig, Online article 'Apollo and the Van Allen Belts.' This article has recently been difficult to find. Check out his website at www.braeunig.us or refer to Jarrah White and his Moonfaker videos as he counters Braeunig's claims regarding the Van Allen belts.

[14] Dr. James A. Van Allen, 'Radiation Belts around the Earth,' Scientific American, published March, 1959

[15] Barbara B. Poppe and Kristen P. Jorden, Sentinels of the Sun: Forecasting Space Weather, p. 71-72.

[16] Ibid., p. 72.

[17] Article 'NASA's Van Allen Probes Discover a Surprise Circling Earth', www.nasa.gov

Chapter Five

Shielding for Radiation, Thermal Control, and Micrometeoroids

Some Tinfoil Should Do It!

As Chapter 4 has shown, the Apollo spacecraft had inadequate shielding for the radiation it would have encountered in the Van Allen belts, GCRs, SPEs, and CMEs. Also, as discussed in that chapter, the August 4, 1972 SPE had an intensity of 960 rems, that is, depending on your source. To attenuate 960 rems to 40 rems, an amount considered acceptable levels for the astronauts, the Apollo spacecraft would have needed approximately four inches of aluminum shielding. That's still a high level of radiation to be exposed to when encountering an SPE, given that the dosage accumulated would have depended on the duration the astronauts had been exposed to this intense radiation.

Note: The standard allowable dosage for employees working with radioactive materials is 5 rems per year. Given the real possibility that the Apollo astronauts would have encountered an SPE, and that NASA says the CM shielding would have attenuated radiation down to approximately 40 rems, that's still a dose of radiation equivalent to eight times the allowable yearly dosage as set by governmental regulatory agencies. However, the duration of exposure to 40 rems needs to be taken into consideration. The fact that there would have been substantial damage incurred by the astronauts remained uncontested. The main point being, that no one, not even experts can talk in definitive terms regarding terrestrial and extraterrestrial radiation and its effects on people, especially those that were part of the Apollo missions beyond LEO.

John H. Mauldin has a Masters in Physics and a PhD in Science Education and is also a former employee of NASA. His responsibilities included work on the Voyager missions. He made some interesting remarks about the required protection from radiation for manned missions.

Mauldin writes:

> By comparison, solar flares can deliver GeV protons in the same energy range as most cosmic particles but at much higher intensities. Increase of energy accounts for most of the increased radiation danger because GeV protons or their products will penetrate several meters of material.[1]

As for GCRs:

> Cosmic particles are dangerous, come from all sides, and require at least 2 meters of shielding around all living organisms.[2]

Proponents of the Apollo missions have pointed out that Mauldin is talking about interstellar travel and that the enormous distances between solar systems are far greater than interplanetary travel, therefore requiring more shielding than is needed for manned missions to the Moon and to Mars. Therefore, the proponents are insinuating that radiation intensities are different, depending on the area of space that a mission is travelling through. That insinuation is partly true, but it does not represent the whole picture.

Are SPEs any different in intensities between the Earth, Moon and Mars? One could argue correctly that SPEs are more intense between the Earth and the Moon, given their closer proximity to the Sun. In fact, when talking about SPEs, Mauldin points out that SPEs "can give a dose of hundreds to thousands of rem over a few hours at a distance of miles from Earth." No one needs to be an expert to know what "hundreds to thousands of rem" over a few hours can do to a human being. And as shown in Chapter 4, NASA tends to give the impression that by calling space between the Earth and Moon 'cislunar space,' the elements that could be encountered by manned missions to the Moon is somehow less intense than 'deep space' manned missions, which is not entirely accurate.

Are GCRs any different in intensities inside and outside of our solar system? GCRs are no less dangerous in our solar system, even when we factor in the solar cycle of the Sun. In fact, when it comes to shielding spacecraft, especially on manned missions anywhere in 'cislunar space' and beyond, it is the mass and density of the material that is the important factor in protecting the astronauts.

Ralph Rene writes:

> It wouldn't matter if the shielding material was made of lead or not. Radiation shielding depends mostly on the mass and density of the material that is between the source and the victim. Lead is effective because of its high density. On an equal basis a layer of water is even more effective, despite its lighter mass, but lead is less bulky.[3]

Of course, to launch a spacecraft shielded by the added weight of water or lead, would far exceed the lift capabilities of any rocket design in existence. And as we discussed in Chapter 2, the heavy lift capabilities of the Saturn V, the most powerful rocket designed and built as is claimed by NASA, couldn't even make it to LEO because of its unstable F-1 engines.

> Aluminium shielding thickness is most effective at stopping primary heavy nuclei, the type of cosmic radiation that causes the most damage to living tissue.

> Components of the annual cosmic-ray dose equivalent vs. shielding thickness are shown below at a time of minimum solar activity. High energy protons interact with shielding material to generate additional secondary particles. With about 7.5 cm of aluminium, the normal dose equivalent is reduced from 50 rem to 35 rem. Calculations for a very large solar flare series, like events of August 1972, show that the lethal unshielded dose of about 1000 rem is reduced to 40 rem with 9 cm of aluminium shielding.[4]

As has been made clear, the Apollo CM, and particularly the LM, had nowhere near the shielding necessary to attenuate radiation to 40 rems. However, the CM might have had the protection it needed, had it stayed in the relative safety of LEO well under the Van Allen belts and with some protection of the Earth's magnetic shield. So, the only protection the CM and LM would have had with an SPE like the intensity of the August 4, 1972 SPE, is to avoid it and given the level of technology used in the Apollo missions, that would have been impossible.

NASA said it had procedures for the astronauts to follow in the event of an emergency, like encountering an SPE.

For example:

> A radiation-survey meter (RSM) is taken on each Apollo mission. The RSM is a direct-reading dose-rate instrument that allows the crewmen to determine radiation levels in any desired location in their compartment. The crewmen would use the RSM to find a habitable low-dose region within the spacecraft in the event of a radiation emergency.[5]

When one checks out the actual dimensions of the crew compartment in both the CM and LM, one wonders where exactly, "a habitable low-dose region within the spacecraft in the event of a radiation emergency" would be located.

Aside from exposures to the Van Allen belts, GCRs, SPEs and CMEs, the Apollo spacecraft would also have had to contend with thermal control and micrometeoroids. For thermal control, there's still a debate as to the best methods for controlling spacecraft temperatures while in LEO and beyond, although seemingly, this debate was resolved during the Apollo missions. And as is common knowledge, micrometeoroids can be a hazard to any space mission, whether manned or unmanned. With inadequate shielding, a high velocity object in space can penetrate a spacecraft with catastrophic consequences, in addition to what it would do to an astronaut on an extra vehicular activity (EVA). We will be discussing Thermal control and micrometeoroid protection in this chapter.

Any one of these six space environmental elements, the Van Allen belts, GCRs, SPEs, CMEs, thermal control and micrometeoroids, could have ended a mission in minutes or even seconds, let alone encountering all six of these elements at once. Thus, to appreciate the complexity and seriousness of any of these elements in the space environment, we must first review the shielding of both the CSM and LM. As you read on, it'll become evident that neither the CSM or LM had anywhere near the protection needed for any of the elements of the space environment as mentioned above.

Command And Service Module Dimensions And Shielding

The CSM consisted of two sections, the SM and CM. The SM was 24.93 feet in length with a diameter of 12.79 feet. It was made of one-inch thick walls comprised of aluminum alloy honeycomb panels. It was divided into six compartments, four of which carried the propellent needed for the 20,500-pound thrust Service Propulsion System (SPS) engine. The fifth compartment contained the fuel cells and their reactants needed for electrical power, life support systems, water management and air temperature regulation. On Apollo 11, the sixth compartment was left empty. On later missions, the sixth compartment was used to carry the Scientific Instrument Module (SIM). The SM also carried most of the communications as well as the Reaction Control System for attitude control. The aluminum alloy honeycomb panels would have needed to protect the propellants and communications equipment from all of the six space environmental elements mentioned.

The CM had a height of 10.56 feet, with a diameter of 12.82 feet. Its structure consisted of the aft heat shield, the pressurized primary structure or the crew compartment, a central heat shield over the primary structure and a forward heat shield which housed the docking mechanism and the parachutes needed for the eventual splashdown into the Pacific Ocean. The inner pressurized crew compartment was constructed with lightweight double-skinned aluminum alloy material. The non-pressurized central heat shield structure consisted of fiberglass honeycomb, bonded to a steel honeycomb material covering the primary structure. It is this outer layer of the CM that NASA claims provided protection from radiation, thermal, and micrometeoroid exposure. The combined thickness of the materials used to construct the inner and outer walls, was from 1.10 to 1.5 inches thick. There were five windows, all made with triple layers of glass, the outer one being ¾ inches thick. The actual space available to the astronauts was approximately 210 cubic feet, which is about the size of an average car.

The overall protection of the CM consisted of the forward heat shield, the material around the main part of the spacecraft (discussed above), and the aft heatshield. The aft heat shield's primary purpose was to provide protection from the fiery reentry into Earth's atmosphere. The aft heatshield was made of material that charred and burnt away in a process called ablation. The material used in the aft heat shield, was up to 2.5 inches thick.

For the purpose of this chapter, our discussion will focus on the effects of radiation, heat, and micrometeoroid impacts on the CM and LM in cislunar space. The aft heat shield will be discussed in detail in Part 2 of this series.

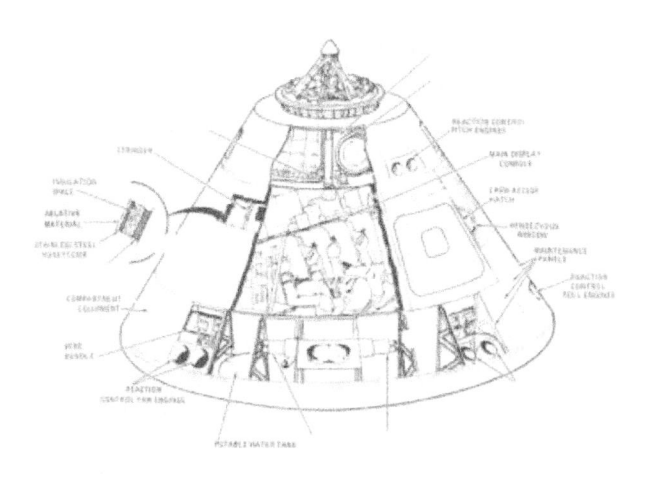

Figure 5.1 – Command Module
Source: NASA

Lunar Module Dimensions And Shielding

Like the CM, the LM had two sections, the descent stage and the ascent stage. The descent stage was approximately 12 feet in diameter and 31 feet diagonally across the landing gear. It was divided into four quadrants which contained the four propellant tanks and the super critical helium tank. It also contained a 10,000-pound thrust engine used for lunar orbit and descent to the lunar surface. The primary structure consisted of aluminum alloy which was also covered with 16 layers of golden Mylar aluminized foil. It is these layers of Mylar aluminized foil around the descent stage, which is supposed to have provided the necessary thermal and micrometeoroid protection.

The ascent stage had a height of 12.34 feet. This contained the crew compartment which had a horizontal shape with a diameter of 7.67 feet and a length of 3.5 feet. It also contained a 3,500-pound thrust engine needed for launch from the lunar surface. The structure consisted of aluminum alloy and had two triangular forward-facing windows and one docking window above the Commander's station. The skin of the LM cabin was just 0.012 inches thick.

> In the end, the lander became a strange mix of strength and fragility. The skin of the descent stage was only a Mylar wrapping stretched over a frame. In the ascent stage, the walls of the crew cabin were thinned down until they were nothing more than a taut aluminum balloon, in some places only five-thousands of an inch thick. Once, a workman accidently dropped a screwdriver inside the cabin and it went through the floor. Now, in space, it seemed deceptively flimsy. When the cabin was pressurized the front hatch bulged outward. *That* had scared John Young, who was in the command module wearing nothing but a pair of long johns; he was up muttering, "I didn't know I was volunteering to go on this damn thing in my underwear…" No wonder Jim McDivitt called his LM "the tissue-paper spacecraft." But it was sturdy enough – even more than enough – for the moon.[6]

Directly over the crew's heads was the hatch that provided access, when docked, to the command module though a tunnel. The crewmen stood in the lunar module, looking forward through a small triangular window on each side, with the commander on the left and the LM pilot on the right. The external skin of both stages was paper-thin aluminum, the lower stage covered by multiple layers of gold Mylar insulation. You could easily poke a pencil through the side of the spacecraft. Portions of the interior were covered with netting to save weight and catch anything that might fall into nooks and crannies inside the LM. Designed to operate only outside the Earth's atmosphere, the LM looked ungainly, had no heat shield, and was incapable of safely entering the Earth's atmosphere.[7]

As you can see from the above section, the Apollo CM had nowhere near the shielding protection necessary to attenuate radiation to acceptable levels. Add to this the windows in both the CM and LM and the overall shielding necessary to protect the astronauts from intense radiation and/or micrometeoroids didn't come close to the level of protection that would have been needed, when compared to what was mentioned above by John Mauldin. The materials used to make the CM walls were 1.5 inches thick which included the aluminum alloy and honeycomb panels. Aside from John Mauldin's recommendation, this doesn't even come close to the four inches of aluminum (or more) that would have been needed to attenuate intense radiation encountered in SPEs, to acceptable levels for the astronauts' safety.

As for the LM, the walls were so thin, you could easily poke any object through them, causing a rapid decompression instantly killing the crew, had they not been wearing their spacesuits. In other words, all that separated the two astronauts in the LM from that of the vacuum of space were cabin walls equivalent to the thickness of three layers of kitchen foil.

The LM and its flimsy design, will be discussed in detail in Part 2 of the series.

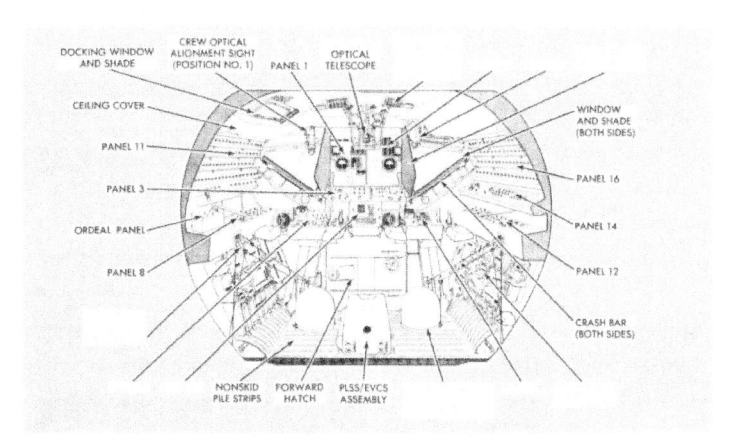

Figure 5.2 – Lunar Module. Notice there are no seats. This was by design to save weight. The two astronauts had to stand during descent and ascent from lunar surface
Source: NASA

In the next section, we'll discuss the issue of temperature in space including whether it's hot, cold, or neither and why the importance of thermal control would have been another necessary aspect for any of the Apollo missions to have succeeded.

Temperature In Space

We often hear about the extreme coldness of space and how anything exposed to this environment will freeze. That's not entirely accurate in our area of space. Earth's atmosphere diffuses heat more evenly because of conduction and convection. But the vacuum of space for the most part is devoid of matter, so therefore it can be better described as neither cold nor hot.

Being that the Earth and Moon are approximately 93 million miles from the Sun, the effects of temperature are a constant threat for space missions in LEO and beyond. In LEO, spacecraft would spend half their orbits exposed to the Sun with temperatures on the outside of the hull reaching as high as +200 degrees Celsius, while reaching -200 degrees Celsius in LEO away from the Sun. But in cislunar space, the spacecraft would be constantly exposed to the Sun, increasing temperatures on one side of the hull. In addition, the area of space around the spacecraft would act like an insulator, adding to the problem of heat buildup within the crew compartment.

The analogy of a thermos flask best illustrates the problem. The area between the inner and outer sections of the thermos flask is devoid of any of the outside atmosphere, in effect, a vacuum. Therefore, heat in the inner section cannot be conducted outside, keeping hot liquids close to the same temperature for hours. This can be compared to the vacuum of space around the spacecraft. The spacecraft would lose heat through radiation, much like the thermos flask. So, in effect, the vacuum around the spacecraft becomes an insulator.

> Here's what's going on: Most of the gas in space is too thin to warm anything up. Essentially, there are not enough gas particles to "bump" into and transfer heat to an object. So if you were in space, but shielded from the sun, you would radiate away nearly all your heat quickly and cool to the cosmic background temperature. Step (or float) into the sun, and you'd be warmed. Either way you'd need lots of protection![8]

If the Apollo missions had really circumnavigated the Moon, the problem would have been to prevent the CM and LM from getting too hot, not too cold. The Apollo spacecraft would constantly have been bombarded by the Sun's rays on one side of the outside hull enroute to the Moon, with the same conditions on the way back to Earth, reaching temperatures as high as +200 degrees Celsius or more. The opposite side of the CM and/or LM would have been cold by comparison since the vacuum of space cannot conduct heat from the side facing the Sun. In addition to this, the CM crew compartment atmosphere, would have acted like a conductor heating all areas of the CM interior.

Although there would have been heat loss though radiation on both sides of the CM and LM, the constant bombardment of the Sun's rays would have been a constant source of heat, causing a buildup of temperatures to dangerous levels that would have eventually killed the astronauts. As the above quote says, "Step (or float) into the sun, and you'd be warmed. Either way you'd need lots of protection!"

However, NASA says that it solved this problem through environmental and thermal control.

The environmental and thermal control aspects of any spacecraft, depends on whether its mission is in LEO or beyond. For the purposes of this book, we'll discuss the thermal control aspects of the Apollo missions in the area of space between the Earth and Moon that is, cislunar space.

The Apollo Spacecraft Environmental And Thermal Control

Deflecting, radiating, and regulating the temperature from the Sun's heat as well as heat produced from inside the CM would not only have been imperative for the safety of the astronauts, it would have been essential for the proper functioning of the power systems of the Apollo spacecraft. The instruments and computers, for both the CM and LM, would have needed to be maintained at a temperature conducive to the astronauts' safety.

Since conduction and convection are absent in the vacuum of space, the thermal control system had to be designed to reject the excess heat into space, while maintaining appropriate temperatures inside the Apollo spacecraft for all phases of the mission. Therefore, this along with many other considerations, would needed to have been factored into the design of the CM and LM. A malfunction of the environmental and thermal control system alone would have ended any of the Apollo missions in hours, possibly minutes. Hence, considering the vast distances between the Earth and Moon for our level of technology, there would have been no possibility of an Apollo mission making it back to Earth safely, in the event of an environmental and thermal control system failure. In LEO, the astronauts may have survived a partial failure of the environmental and thermal control system in the CM, where emergency procedures could at least be implemented for re-entry and an eventual splash down.

The Atmosphere Revitalization System and the Thermal Control System is another of the many aspects of the Apollo CM and LM that would have had to work to near perfection, since, as we've previously established, there is little or no redundancy in the design.

Atmosphere Revitalization System

The Atmosphere Revitalization System (ARS) was to have regulated the temperatures from the heat produced inside the CM. For example, heat produced from the instruments and components necessary for the proper function of the spacecraft would have needed to be radiated and/or routed to mechanisms that would have rejected the heat to the vacuum of space. Carbon dioxide and humidity produced by the astronauts would needed to have been removed too. All of this would have had to be done on a continuous basis.

The ARS involved heat exchangers, electrical heaters, and water glycol coolant loops. The heat exchangers were used to heat the crew compartment if needed, with electrical heaters used as backup for more heat if necessary. To help regulate the temperatures for astronaut safety as well as for the proper functioning of the CM and LM, coolant loops would have cooled the electronics. This excess heat was then routed to radiators in the Service Module and emitted through radiation out into space. This, of course, is how the ARS was supposed to have worked according to the few NASA documents still available.

Thermal Control System

The Thermal Control System (TCS) was used to help regulate and deflect heat, mainly from external sources, such as the Sun. The design of the Apollo spacecraft TCS included Mylar foil coating applied to most of the surfaces of the CM and LM. The Mylar foil coatings helped to deflect heat from the Sun's solar rays. However, degradation of the thermal coatings would have needed to be factored in on any of the Apollo missions since long-term working solutions for these coatings had yet to be found. The boost protective cover over the main CM structure helped to protect the thermal coating during launch, which was then jettisoned before orbital insertion. But given the unpredictability and variations of the harsh environment of space, calculations needed to be precise, since any estimates would have been inadequate. Any encounter with one of the six space environmental elements, would have required immediate action on the part of the astronauts, although GCRs would have constituted a constant threat. This would have required the response time of an autonomous computer equipped with sensors capable of determining the degradation or damage done to the protective coating and/or shielding and then communicating that information to the astronauts. Of course, as has been established in Chapter 3, the AGC did not have this capability.

As one side of the CM and LM would have been facing the Sun enroute to the Moon, a method had to be devised to even out the heat around the CM and LM's hull.

> To prevent one side of the spacecraft roasting and the opposite side freezing in the constant sunlight of cislunar space, it was oriented with its principal axis perpendicular to the ecliptic, then set on a 20-minute cycle for passive thermal control (PTC) in a regime more popularly known as the barbecue mode. This had to be established before the astronauts could retire for the night.[9]

After launch into LEO of the Saturn V, it wouldn't have been long before the CM had fired its engine for TLI into cislunar space. So, if Passive Thermal Control (PTC) was necessary to help even out the temperature of the CM, one wonders why this needed to be "established before the astronauts could retire for the night" and not before since it would not have taken long for the CM to heat up owing to the constant rays of the Sun shortly after leaving LEO. But PTC was hardly a solution to the problem of protecting the CM from the constant heat of the Sun, and given the degradation process of the reflective Mylar covering of the outer hull, this further exposed the CM to extreme heat.

The slow roll of the CM and docked LM along its longitudinal axis for PTC also had its own problems. PTC supposedly worked well during the Apollo 8 mission. But according to NASA, PTC caused other problems that effected the longitudinal axis of the spacecraft during later Apollo missions since, these missions involved the LM, unlike Apollo 8. This added to further problems in navigation which would have required even more course corrections. Given the tasks of maintaining precise navigation, nothing short of an autonomous computer equipped with sensors interfaced with the navigation and flight control system of the CSM, would have sufficed. As has been established in Chapter 3, crew interface was necessary for making course corrections, which is nowhere near as autonomous as the AGC should have been, aside from the fact that this computer had little or no memory for any of the tasks it was expected to do.

According to NASA:

> The interior of the command module must be protected from the extremes of environment that will be encountered during a mission. These include the heat of boost (up to 1200 degrees F), the cold of space and the heat of the direct rays of the sun (about 280 degrees below zero on the side facing away from the sun and 280 degrees above zero on the other side), and – most critical – the intense temperature of entry (about 5000 degrees F).
>
> The insulation between the inner and outer shells, plus temperature control provided by the environmental control subsystem, protects the crew and sensitive equipment during the CM's long journey in space.[10]

There seems to be more conflicting information regarding the heat outside the CM facing the Sun. As per the above quote NASA indicated it was up to 280 degrees Celsius, while other sources mention 200 degree Celsius. But clearly, NASA is indicating that the Apollo astronauts needed to be protected from the extreme heat of the Sun.

NASA Contradicts Itself, Yet Again

As was discussed in Chapter 3, Apollo 13 had a rupture in one if its oxygen tanks in the SM. As a result, the astronauts had to power down the CSM. This forced the astronauts to move into the LM while coasting back to Earth. However, it is claimed that powering down the CSM caused the temperature to drop within the crew compartment.

> Aboard Odyssey the crew too had been discussing their options. Oxygen tank No 2 was gone – its contents vented to space – but the contents of tank 1 were bleeding away. Jack Swigert was the on-board expert in the CSM systems but all three knew the basics of physics. When the pressure fell to 100lbs/in^2 (689.5kPa) it would be incapable of providing a supply to the fuel cells – or to the cabin. And the temperature too was going down. As Swigert powered down the systems in the Command Module it was getting colder, down already to 58 degrees F (14.4 degrees C) and noticeably chilly.[11]

Now the question is, if the Apollo 13 CM crew compartment became noticeably colder, what about the heat from the Sun's rays that were constantly bombarding the side of the CM and LM? Are we to believe that since there was no heat being produced from the CM's systems after it was powered down, that heat from within the crew compartment was now radiating heat into space faster than the buildup of heat from the Sun's rays? Heat from the Sun that was bombarding the spacecraft hull to temperatures of about 280 degrees Celsius or more? And what about the power systems of the LM? They would have been powered up, so wouldn't they have produced sufficient heat to at least counter some of the heat loss from the CM? If heat from within the CM was radiating at a faster rate than the heat from the Sun, then there wouldn't have been a need for PTC or at least, it should have been slowed down in order to utilize the Sun's rays to warm the CM, since according to NASA, there was concern over the CM's systems getting too cold.

Incredibly though, we are told that Apollo 13 continued with its PTC even when faced with cold temperatures. And even if PTC was slowed or stopped periodically, that raises yet another issue. Given that the LM was now vital to the astronauts' survival and would have remained docked to the CM for most of the mission back to Earth. The fact that the LM structure had even less protection for the astronauts than that of the CM (the LM walls having the thickness of three layers of kitchen foil), PTC (according to NASA) would have been a reasonable method for the LM. But now, this would have been counterproductive for the CM, since the CM and LM were docked for most of the Apollo 13 mission.

Thus for Apollo 13, PTC works for one spacecraft, but not the other spacecraft docked to it. Therefore, once again, NASA contradicts itself.

PTC Would Not Have Worked

As has been discussed so far, the CM and LM had nowhere near the protection necessary for any one of the six elements that could have been encountered in cislunar space. And, in fact, PTC would not have been a solution to the problem of evening out the heat from the Sun around the hull of the CM and LM either.

> Ironically, that 'Barbecue Mode' we mentioned earlier – rotating the unprotective craft – actually would have ensured that the Apollo astronauts were like chickens on a spit: cooked, fried, baked, radiated (call it what you will) on all sides! The crew would have been better protected from solar radiation by not rotating the CSM and using an appropriate shield on the sunward side of the craft.[12]

Therefore, since PTC isn't an effective way of evening out heat around the spacecraft, then the ARS and TCS would not have functioned as they were designed to. One system has to compliment the other, or the whole system fails.

As for the equivalent of three layers of kitchen foil surrounding the LM and whatever protection NASA claims it offered, would have led to a disaster by any of the astronauts accidently putting his foot through one of the side panels.

NASA Reveals It Knew Little About The Space Environment

During testing, it was discovered that extreme temperatures could have damaged the heat shield making a safe re-entry into Earth's atmosphere impossible. This was discussed during the Apollo 13 mission after one of the oxygen tanks ruptured.

> There were other considerations too. Jettisoning the Service Module would expose the base of the Command Module to an untested environment. Although the heat shield embraced the entire exterior of the conical structure, the main defence against frictional heating on re-entry was the convex base. To expose that to the extreme temperatures of space would be unwise and risky. Moreover, nobody knew

what effect jettisoning the Service Module would have on the Command Module. Better to be close to home when that event was necessary, just before entering the atmosphere.[13]

From the quote we learn of NASA's concern about exposing the "Command Module to an untested environment." However, this "untested environment" was supposed to have been determined during the testing phase of the CM's heat shield in NASA's vacuum chamber which is supposed to have been able to simulate most conditions of space. But if NASA was really so concerned about this "untested environment," then it shouldn't have sent any manned mission without first testing an unmanned Apollo mission beyond LEO to circumnavigate the Moon.

NASA claims to have completed nine successful manned missions beyond LEO, six of which landed on the lunar surface, while admitting their knowledge of cislunar space was limited.

Micrometeoroid Shielding

This chapter has already revealed the inadequate shielding provided for many of the elements in the space environment for the Apollo astronauts which was also included provisions for shielding from micrometeoroids. And, as has been established, the LM had far less protection than that of the CM. Further, when looking into the data regarding micrometeoroid shielding, again we find incomplete information and/or missing documents.

Given that space missions, manned or unmanned, were in their infancy in the 1960s and 1970s and little or nothing was known about the elements of the space environment talked about in this book, NASA further realized that it needed to address the issue of micrometeoroids.

A micrometeoroid impact alone, would have been disastrous for any Apollo mission. With the shielding used in the CM and LM there was no redundancy. Any failure of one aspect of the Apollo spacecraft shielding, would have meant an abrupt end to any mission.

NASA launched a series of satellites called the Pegasus missions to collect data on the thermal effects on coating surfaces, radiation effects on instruments and micrometeoroid impacts. There are no long-term solutions to the effects of the thermal environment coating applied to spacecraft hulls, as has been established in Chapter 4. NASA didn't have the equipment necessary to detect radiation intensities beyond a certain level, further eroding the mylar coating on the spacecraft hull. We'll now concentrate on the Pegasus missions' main purpose, which was to collect data on micrometeoroid impacts.

The Pegasus Missions

NASA launched three satellites in the Pegasus missions' program on the Saturn I rocket along with a boilerplate CSM (non-functioning CSM). The boilerplate Apollo spacecraft were used in numerous tests on the ground as well as in LEO. Of the boilerplate CSMs launched to LEO, three of them were used for the Pegasus satellites which were located in the empty Service Module.

- The first Pegasus satellite was launched with Apollo 9 (SA-9) on February 16, 1965,
- The second was launched with Apollo 8 (SA-8) on May 25, 1965, and

- The third was launched with Apollo 10 (SA-10) on July 30, 1965.

Note: Apollo 9 (SA-9) was launched first due to a delay with Apollo 8 (SA-8).

These missions are not to be confused with the later manned missions of Apollos 8, 9 and 10.

In Earth orbit, the Pegasus satellites extended its folded arrays which reached approximately 95 feet in length. The arrays were designed for detecting and collecting data on micrometeoroid impacts and there were additional sample protective shields that were mounted on the arrays. These sample protective shields were designed to be retrieved from a manned mission for further detailed analysis. The design and data from these sample protective shields, were to be incorporated into the shielding of the Apollo missions.

The whole point of the Pegasus missions was to gain data in support of the Apollo Moon missions. However, the Pegasus missions went no higher than a 500 miles orbit which meant that they were nowhere near the area of cislunar space in which the Apollo missions would have spent the bulk of their time. Data from within 500 miles in Earth orbit would not have sufficed for missions planning a 480,000-mile round trip. That's an area of cislunar space covering millions of square miles.

Moving The Goal Posts

The sample protective shields installed on the Pegasus arrays were to be retrieved by one of the manned Gemini missions but were not for reasons never explained. Although data from sensors was obviously stored, vital information from any retrieval of these panels was lost.

NASA worked on a probability basis which is the norm in a lot of industries, for example aircraft manufactures. But by the 1960s, aircraft manufactures had decades of research and data to use as a probability factor. However, at the time of the Apollo Moon program, NASA had at best, several years of research and data for its manned space program. So, the probability factor for manned space missions in an unfamiliar environment with such little research and data becomes more of an educated guess at best.

> The original failure criterion for the SPS propellant tanks was perforation of the SM honeycomb skin panels. Because the failure criterion was too stringent to meet the desired probability of mission success, engineers considered an alternative. If the original criterion had remained, the test shown in figure 4 would have been an SPS tank failure.[14]

This quote is an indication of the strategy NASA used. If the criterion was too stringent for the mission's success, NASA changed the criterion, hence moving the goal posts. This is a strategy prevalent with much of the technology used in the Apollo Moon missions, some of which have been shown in this book.

Summary

- We learned that the Apollo CM had nowhere near the shielding required for the radiation that would have been encountered in cislunar space, according to former NASA employee and physicist John H. Mauldin.

- The level of shielding for the LM was even less than that of the CM, with walls equivalent to three layers of kitchen foil.

- Contrary to what we are told, cislunar space is not cold. Given the Earth and Moon's proximity to the Sun, cislunar space could be considered quite warm, given that objects such as spacecraft are directly in the path of the Sun's rays. In fact, the challenge for the CM and LM would have been to prevent them from getting too hot.

- We've learned that the ARS in the CM was inadequate since NASA's method of PTC, would not have properly evened out the heat from the Sun.

- We learned too that in Apollo 13, both the docked CM and LM temperature control was in conflict, since given the circumstances for that mission, PTC would have supposedly worked for the LM, but not the CM, which is another NASA contradiction.

- During the Apollo 13 mission, NASA expressed concern about exposing the CM heatshield to an "untested environment" revealing it knew little or nothing about cislunar space.

- NASA launched three satellites called the Pegasus missions to collect data on micrometeoroid impacts. These three missions had an Earth orbital height of no more than 500 miles. The area of cislunar space is millions of square miles, so the Pegasus missions' data collection, would have been scant at best.

- We also learned that when the criterion for testing technology during the Apollo program was too stringent, NASA lowered the requirements. In effect, they wrote the rules to fit the Apollo Moon missions' script.

As we've learned in Chapters 2, 3, 4, and now 5, NASA lacked the technology and in-depth knowledge of cislunar space, to send any manned missions beyond LEO.

Chapter 5 - Endnotes

[1] John H. Mauldin, Prospects For Interstellar Travel, p. 225.

[2] Ibid., p. 225.

[3] Ralph Rene, NASA Mooned America, p.129.

[4] 'Aerospace America' paper published October 1987.

[5] Robert A. English, Richard E. Benson, J. Vernon Baily, and Charles M. Barnes, NASA TN D-7080 Apollo Experience Report-Protection Against Radiation, pp. 8-9.

[6] Andrew Chaikin, A Man On The Moon The Voyages Of The Apollo Astronauts, p. 156.

[7] Gene Kranz, Failure Is Not An Option Mission Control From Mercury To Apollo 13 And Beyond, p. 215.

[8] 'What's the Temperature of Outer Space?', www.space.com

[9] David M. Harland, The First Men On The Moon The Story of Apollo 11, p. 153.

[10] www.history.nasa.gov/alsj/CSM06_Command_Module_Overdrive_pp39-52.pdf. {p. 42.}

[11] David Baker, NASA MISSION AS – 508 APOLLO 13 1970 (including the Saturn V, CM – 109, SM – 109, LM – 7) Owners' Workshop Manual, p.77.

[12] Mary Bennett and David S. Percy, Dark Moon Apollo And The Whistle-Blowers, p.101.

[13] Op Cit., Baker, P. 85.

[14] Michael D. Bjorkman, Eric L. Christiansen, America's Moon Landing Program Apollo Meteoroid Shielding Design and Analysis at the Manned Spacecraft Center, p. 23.

Chapter 6

Conclusion

14,000 Apollo 11 Telemetry Tapes are Missing!

Don't worry, no one will notice.

Several years ago, former NASA engineer James Oberg described the act of questioning the Apollo Moon missions as "cultural vandalism." James Oberg speaks several languages and is no doubt an intelligent individual, so you'd expect he would refrain from making such comments and instead, use erudition to make his point. I believe his remarks were made in reference to author Ralph Rene and his book 'NASA Mooned America.' Proponents tend to resort to these types of comments, since NASA has either lost or destroyed a lot of its own purported evidence.

Missing And/Or Destroyed Documents

Throughout my research into the Apollo Moon missions, I've repeatedly come across missing and/or destroyed documents as well as incomplete information in general.

You may have similar challenges finding information on the space environment, e.g. 'James Van Allen's research into the radiation belts', most of which can only be found at the University of Iowa. Further, some of this information is subject to copyright rules. Yet, this information regarding the radiation belts effects our climate and contributes to climate change and therefore, should be the property of every human being on this planet. However, as we discussed in Chapter 4, it is impossible to detect the true intensity of the radiation belts with our level of technology, so as of right now, data regarding the radiation belts, is a moot subject. And what information does exist, is subject to conflicts and contradictions.

Regarding the management of the meteoroid risk assessment for the CM and LM:

> Evidence does not show that Headquarters or the MSC ASPO ever managed the meteoroid risk for the Apollo program as a whole. However, it is possible to estimate the overall system risk from the available data.[1]

If there's no evidence as to what aspect of the Apollo Moon program managed the meteoroid risk assessment, then this is just another way of saying, the documents are missing. Therefore, it's left up to the researcher "to estimate the overall system risk from the available data."

In talking about the protective thermal shielding, the authors had this to say about the ablator material on the CM:

> Many of the details of the ablator design were classified confidential at the time and hence are missing from the unclassified meteoroid impact analysis reports.[2]

Considering that the Apollo missions took place 50 years ago, there's no need to keep these documents classified. What the above quote really means, is once again, more missing documents.

Don Pettit is a NASA astronaut who was on three missions, two on the ISS and one on the Space Shuttle. He had this to say about the possibility of any future manned mission to the Moon:

> I'd go to the Moon in a nanosecond. The problem is we don't have the technology to do that anymore. We used to, but we destroyed that technology and it's a painful process to build it back again.[3]

The reader will recall in Chapter 4, a YouTube video posted in the last couple of years, with NASA engineer Kelly Smith talking about the need to solve the problem of protecting astronauts from radiation within the Van Allen Belts, before sending any manned missions through them. Now we have NASA astronaut Don Pettit, who admits that all the technology for the Apollo Moon missions has been destroyed. Losing these documents is one thing, but to destroy them is another. A deliberate act to destroy this evidence means there is something that was not meant to be seen by the public since this 'evidence' either proved the impossibility of manned missions to the Moon, or this 'evidence' never existed.

What's left of this 'evidence' should be readily accessible to the public and it should be easy to find, but it's not. Instead, Apollo spacecraft schematics, data, transcripts, photos, films, documents and any other purported evidence that relates to the Apollo Moon missions, is scattered on several websites. Of course, you'll find some of the Apollo missions' documents on the MSFC and NASA's websites, but they're usually buried under thousands of unrelated documents. And as was reported in Chapter 2, any documents you do find are often incomplete or no longer exist. Ideally, NASA should have had one archive building and one website dedicated to preserving all of the Apollo Moon missions' hardware and documentation, with a virtual road map detailing where to find any of the documents for the interested reader or researcher. And in this digital age, all of the documentation could have been preserved for posterity as well as a blueprint for future manned missions beyond LEO. This now seems to be an impossible feat, according to NASA astronaut Don Pettit.

Aside from the missing and incomplete documents, there is the claim that if there was a conspiracy involved in the Apollo Moon missions, then some of the 400,000 people involved in the Apollo program, would have come forward by now and revealed the hoax. The hierarchical structure in projects such as the Apollo manned space program, is designed so that everyone and their expertise are leveraged on a need-to-know basis. It's a system of compartmentalization that is used regularly to control the flow of information, where a contractor in one region of the country would have had no idea whether a specific part they designed and/or manufactured for the CM or LM, actually made it into LEO or beyond. For that matter, they wouldn't have known whether the actual CM or LM itself, went anywhere near LEO or beyond, as they would have had to rely on the same news sources as everyone else.

Therefore, when it comes to the Apollo missions' documents or any direct or related information in general, it's left up to the researcher to try and find as much information on the Apollo Moon missions as possible. But this proves to be an arduous task, since with each passing decade, this information continues to disappears into oblivion.

The Missing Or Destroyed Saturn V Documents

Dwayne A. Day:

> Much of the technical design documentation for the Saturn 5 and the Apollo spacecraft has indeed been lost or destroyed. In fact, much of it was never saved, nor meant to be saved. Certainly, there are hundreds of thousands of pages of technical documentation preserved on microfilm and in boxes at the National Archives facility near Atlanta. But these records (I've seen them) are incomplete, and they contain considerable gaps. There is nothing close to a complete set of "Saturn blueprints" in the federal archives. I have

also been to the archives at Kennedy Space Centre, Marshall Space Flight Center, Houston, and Forth Worth. There is nothing approaching a "complete set of Saturn 5 blueprints" anywhere.[4]

This quote further confirms that most of the documents were in fact destroyed. This is one of many troubling and disturbing aspects of the Apollo Moon mission program.

Note: The title of the article from which the above quote is taken, is not to be misconstrued as the author Dwayne A. Day is a proponent of the Apollo missions. Day goes through great lengths to justify why the Saturn V documents were either "lost or destroyed," which makes for some amusing and interesting reading. However, I ask the reader to consider the significance of not preserving all of the detailed documentation regarding 'man's greatest scientific accomplishment of the 20th century.

Missing Apollo 11 Telemetry Tapes

By now, we have a sense of what is lost when it comes to the missing and/or destroyed documents. But the most disturbing of all, are the missing or erased 14,000, 14-inch canister reels of telemetry tapes from the Apollo 11 mission, as reported by Reuters on July 16, 2009.

The Apollo 11 telemetry tapes contained three pieces of vital information:

- The biomedical data of the Apollo astronauts
- The telemetry from the Apollo spacecraft performance
- The visual signal of the first two astronauts to walk on the lunar surface, Neil Armstrong and Buzz Aldrin

To understand the significance of these tapes and how seemingly impossible it would have been to have lost them, I've provided a brief history below.

Telemetry From The Moon

Hundreds of millions of people around the world tuned in to watch the first Apollo astronauts walk on the Moon via live television. The signal of the film images from the Moon was first sent to tracking stations in Australia, Spain, and California. These images were then sent up to the Intelsat satellite in Earth orbit and then finally to Mission Control in Houston. From Houston, the signal was sent to the main television networks for broadcast.

Hence, the signal of the Apollo 11 astronauts walking on the lunar surface, wasn't exactly live television after all.

NASA had only budgeted for 500 kHz of bandwidth, which was far less than the 4.5 MHz used by the television industry back then. This created a problem, as the bandwidth signals didn't match. A solution had to be found before images from the lunar surface could be broadcast on American television.

> To cope with this reduction in bandwidth, NASA hired the Westinghouse Electric Corporation in Baltimore, Md., to develop a special television camera that used a non-standard scan format of 10 frames per second and 320 lines of resolution, compared with the U.S. television standard of 30 frames per second and 525 lines.[5]

Furthermore, a converter was needed to adapt the slow scan format of the Apollo 11 film.

> Because commercial television could not broadcast the slow-scan format, NASA hired the RCA Corporation to build a scan converter to optically and electronically adapt these images to a standard U.S. broadcast TV signal. The tracking stations converted the signal and transmitted them by way of microwave links, Intelsat communications satellites, and AT&T analog landlines to Mission Control in Houston. By the time the images appeared on international television, they were substantially degraded.[6]

This is the degraded film version of Neil Armstrong and Buzz Aldrin walking on the lunar surface that hundreds of millions of people watched around the world. Copies of this degraded film were made and transferred to VHS videos in the 1970s and 1980s, but since the source for this film has now disappeared, it cannot be authenticated.

Once the Apollo 11 signal was converted for U.S. broadcast, the 14,000 reels of telemetry tapes were stored in metal cannisters, placed in boxes and shipped by airfreight to the Goddard Space Flight Center (GSFC). After the telemetry tapes were reviewed by GSFC personnel, the telemetry tapes were shipped to the Washington National Records Center (WNRC). It is from the WNRC that the telemetry tapes have mysteriously disappeared sometime within the last few decades or more, but no one really knows for sure, or so we were led to believe.

In the official report about the missing Apollo 11 telemetry tapes, (which can be found on NASA's website) NASA has referred to the tapes as "backup tapes." This NASA report was written nearly forty years after the Apollo 11 mission, so it's clear that by using the term "backup tapes," NASA is trying to diminish the historical significance of these telemetry tapes, since they are now missing.

However, the significance of the telemetry tapes cannot be overstated.

Here is a great example of the significance of these tapes:

As has been reported by Apollo Moon hoax researcher Bart Sibrel, when Ron Howard asked NASA for the telemetry tapes for his documentary commemorating the 40th anniversary of the first Apollo Moon landing, he was politely informed by NASA that the telemetry tapes have disappeared.

Howard wanted to format the film of the astronauts on the Moon to IMAX, but he first needed the original master tapes, i.e. the telemetry tapes to do so. Therefore, Howard had to settle for old VHS copies of the astronauts on the Moon for his 40th commemoration documentary.

Figure 6.1 – An example of telemetry tapes used by NASA during the Apollo missions. Each reel is 14" wide. There were 14,000 reels containing data from Apollo 11
Source: NASA

In the meantime, a frantic search from former NASA personnel had been underway for the missing Apollo 11 telemetry tapes. This is where the story gets even more interesting.

Missing, Destroyed, Or Never Existed, Take Your Pick

The search for the telemetry tapes began in 1997, when a British author contacted John Sarkissian, an operations scientist of the Parkes Radio Observatory in Australia about his role in the Apollo 11 mission. For three years, he searched for the Apollo 11 telemetry tapes, with no success. Then in 2002, John Saxon, an operations supervisor at the Honeysuckle Creek tracking station in Australia, which also tracked Apollo 11, claims that while he was at a reunion picnic, another Honeysuckle Creek tracking station retiree (identity not revealed in the NASA report) brought along a magnetic tape canister which he dubbed from the original M-22 recording of Apollo 11.

Some of the proponents claim this magnetic cannister is 'proof' that the Apollo 11 telemetry tapes were eventually found. Just how much information do the proponents think is on this <u>one</u> telemetry tape anyway? Each 14-inch telemetry tape had about 15 minutes of data on it and there were 14,000 reels of telemetry tapes for Apollo 11. So how is this one magnetic tape proof that the Apollo 11 telemetry tapes were found? Further, the retiree says he kept the telemetry tape for 36 years in the garage of his Canberra home and brought it to a reunion picnic in 2002. But the math doesn't add up, as Apollo 11 took place in 1969 and he brought the telemetry tape to the reunion picnic in 2002. This adds up to is 33 years since the Apollo 11 mission. So, was this one telemetry tape connected to the Apollo 11 mission? As will be seen shortly, it was not.

Meanwhile back in the United States, Bill Wood, a retired senior engineer at the Goldstone tracking station in California, which also tracked Apollo 11, started his own search for the telemetry tapes. While Wood was searching, Richard Nafzger, who oversaw the television processing during the Apollo 11 mission, provided access to the one remaining analog machine capable of playing the slow-scan telemetry tapes for the recently found magnetic canister provided by our mysterious retiree.

Note: I have read many comments from the proponents that even if the telemetry tapes are found, it wouldn't matter since there is only one machine left, which needs repair, capable of playing back the telemetry tapes, meaning it would be difficult to access the data. Further, according to the proponents, even if this Apollo 11 data could be accessed, it would be meaningless anyway. This sort of reasoning is one of many in a long list of desperate attempts to justify the missing telemetry tapes.

The telemetry tape provided by the retiree was fed into the machine and turned out to have nothing on it but chatter and simulation from 1967. There was nothing at all related to the Apollo 11 mission. In the meantime, the search continued for the thousands of missing reels of telemetry tapes at the WNRC.

Wikipedia regarding the storing of records in general:

> Those records remain at the WNRC until acceptance as permanent records in the repository, or else they are destroyed and recycled. The records are tracked individually in a database from the time they arrive at the WNRC. While court records are freely available to the public, the majority of records is controlled by their respective originating agency, and all records are subject to the access restrictions to that agency.

In other words, the responsibility for the 14,000 reels of telemetry tapes is not only with the WNRC, but with NASA too. And further, NASA decides who gets access to their documents and/or telemetry tapes and as you'll soon learn, the Apollo 11 telemetry tapes are not missing. They were removed from the WNRC by NASA.

While searching for the missing telemetry tapes, Stan Lebar, a retired Westinghouse Electric program manager, who oversaw the development of the special Apollo 11 camera, received this email from a WNRC employee, dated May 4, 2006:

> This was originally quite an extensive accession in our holdings, 2,614 magnetic tape containers. But over the years, mostly in the 1970s, most of the containers were permanently withdrawn by NASA. Currently, only two containers remain in our possession. Besides the original SF 135, we also have the original charge cards from when the boxes were being withdrawn. Unfortunately, there's very little information on the charge cards beyond the date and the box numbers. Often the name of the person doing the withdrawal is not included, 'NASA Goddard' being written in its place.[7]

In 2007, Richard Nafzger visited the GSFC library and resorts to speculation:

> And then on May 7, 1981, Code 863.1 reported that it needed to procure 164,220 reels of magnetic tape required by the Network Logistics Depot, the Jet Propulsion Laboratory, and three other NASA centers over an eight-month period. Sitting in the library that day, Nafzger could only think, "Wow, it looks like there's a rational connection between the pull out of tapes and the storage of one-inch magnetic tapes. I

> didn't find a smoking gun and they didn't reference the WNRC in name, but they did reference the need for tapes." [8]

What's important here is "they didn't reference the WNRC in name," meaning, there is no documentation as to what magnetic tapes were erased or as is likely, there was no documentation to begin with.

The official NASA report is cleverly written to give the impression that it's all speculation when in actuality, NASA clandestinely removed thousands of Apollo 11 telemetry tapes in the 1970s and either erased or destroyed them. The NASA report insinuates the reason the Apollo 11 telemetry tapes were erased in the 1970s, was because of a shortage of magnetic tapes. But in the same NASA report it shows that this shortage of magnetic tape actually took place in the early 1980s not the 1970s. So that means the Apollo 11 telemetry tapes were either erased or destroyed for other reasons, but not because there was a shortage of magnetic tape. And as we've just seen, there is no documentation as to the NASA individuals who authorized and signed out these telemetry tapes. But at least we know that someone within NASA authorized the removal of the Apollo 11 telemetry tapes from the WNRC, which means the 'missing' tapes should have been no surprise to NASA. However, that's where the paper trail ends.

The whole issue of the 'missing' telemetry tapes is nefarious, to say the least.

As NASA's own report states:

> Without knowing the identity of those responsible for the withdrawal, no one could say what happened or why. The search continued.[9]

So, here's what we know:

- The Apollo 11 telemetry tapes were signed out of the WNRC by NASA in the 1970s.
- The telemetry tapes were deliberately erased or destroyed.
- It wasn't because of a magnetic tape shortage, since this shortage took place a decade later in the 1980s.
- And there are no documents detailing why NASA erased and/or destroyed the telemetry tapes and where the data on the tapes where transferred to.

The obvious question is why were these telemetry tapes erased or destroyed? This is where the real speculation comes in. As there was no shortage of magnetic tapes in the 1970s, then there is only one reason why they were erased or destroyed and that is, because there was never any data from the lunar surface of the Apollo 11 mission to begin with. Therefore, one can only conclude, that the reason NASA destroyed the telemetry tapes was to ensure the hoax was never uncovered.

One of the many arguments put forward is, it doesn't matter if the telemetry tapes were erased or destroyed since all the data was recorded and documented on paper. We leave it up to NASA to set the record straight as to the historical significance of the data on the Apollo 11 telemetry tapes, as opposed to the data being recorded on paper, with a quote from John Saxon in NASA's own report:

> If other tapes are discovered, there may be all sorts of possibilities for space historians and others to study the data from one of the most defining moments in 20th century scientific history.[10]

Translation: The Apollo 11 telemetry tapes are needed for historians to substantiate the data. Without them, there is no data.

No data, no proof. No proof, no Apollo 11 mission.

The Soviets (Russians) To The Rescue, Well maybe

It is said that the Soviets (now Russians) had tracked all of the Apollo Moon missions. If so, then they should have had their own telemetry tapes and since the Americans and Russians are cooperating in their respective manned space program, it's reasonable to assume that Russia would be happy to hand over its telemetry tapes for Apollo 11. Of course, this hasn't happened.

This raises an interesting point since if the Russians knew about the Apollo Moon mission hoax, then surely, they would have said something by now. There are many reasons as to why they didn't, one being they had mishaps in their own manned space program. Another reason for maintaining the secrecy is the leverage they would have had over the decades negotiating with the United States during the Cold War. There will be a more detailed discussion on this in Part 2 of this series.

In Conclusion

50 years after NASA supposedly landed the first men on the Moon, Hollywood finally made the movie they should have made years ago. The movie 'First Man,' is based on the book 'First Man' by James R. Hansen. Of course, I expected the usual glamour from a Hollywood movie, but I was surprised at how little of the actual Moon mission was covered in the movie. The scenes of the Moon landing itself and the

subsequent walking on the lunar surface, were kept to a minimum as well as the lunar liftoff. The voyage back to earth and the re-entry into Earth's atmosphere with the eventual splashdown were left out of the movie entirely. One could argue, the movie 'First Man' was meant to be a biography on Neil Armstrong, so the story was more about him and not the actual mechanics of the Moon landing.

However, being that this movie was about the "First Man" to walk on the lunar surface, it's reasonable to state that the narrative in the movie should have included more of the actual mechanics of the Moon landing itself. But it seems that Hollywood found a convenient way to film the movie without focusing too much on the technology involved. I was planning to write about this movie in Part 2 of the series since it is pertinent to the chapter on the lunar landing and liftoff, but of course, there's really nothing much the movie has to offer. However, I'll refer to NASA's own material as well as the book 'First Man' for a more in-depth analysis of the lunar landing and liftoff.

In "Part 2" of this series, we'll continue on with the official narrative with Apollo 11's journey to lunar orbit, landing and liftoff, as well as the trip back to Earth and re-entry into Earth's atmosphere. Part 2 will include:

- An analysis of the pre-Apollo Moon missions, in preparations for the manned lunar landings.

- How impossible it would have been for the Apollo Moon missions to supposedly have brought back a combined total of 842 pounds of Moon rocks.

- A look at some of the anomalies in the photos and films.

- What technicians at Mission Control in Houston most likely monitored on their computer consoles during the missions.

- The Russian manned space program and possible reasons as to why they didn't reveal the Apollo Moon missions' hoax, then or now.

- And more examples of missing and/or destroyed documents, data, and telemetry tapes.

'Missing evidence' is a prevailing theme throughout the series.

The Apollo Moon missions cost the taxpayers an estimated 150 billion dollars in today's value. NASA still gets approximately 20 billion dollars in funding annually, yet proponents say that NASA needs more funding for its manned space program. However, NASA has spent billions of dollars on unmanned space programs as well as billions more on the ISS. Figures for 2014 show that the United States, Russia, the European Partners, Japan and Canada had spent 150 billion U.S. dollars on the ISS. Of that 150 billion dollars, NASA has contributed the most, approximately 100 billion dollars and continues to contribute an estimated 3 to 4 billion dollars annually.

When you factor in the cost of the ISS and their unmanned space program, it's clear that NASA could have prioritized its funding for its own manned space program capable of not only launch to LEO, but beyond.

An argument often put forward is that the United States Congress appropriates funds to NASA, with directives as to how that funding is to be spent. This indicates NASA has a limited budget for its manned space program. That's not entirely true. All anyone has to do, is to review the annual

Congressional Hearings on NASA funding for insights into this.

NASA really needs to establish just what its priorities are, since manned space missions do not seem to be high on their agenda. In the meantime, NASA relies on history for its legacy established 50 years ago, a legacy that would have you believe:

- Nine Apollo missions and 24 astronauts went beyond LEO and circumnavigated the Moon.
- Six of these Apollo manned missions landed safely on the lunar surface 240,000 miles away.
- All of the Apollo astronauts returned safely to the Earth.
- And many consider this to be the greatest scientific accomplishment of the 20th century.

Here's the reality:

- Since the Apollo Moon missions, there have been no manned space missions outside of LEO.
- In 2011, NASA retired the Space Shuttle, effectively ending its ability to launch its own astronauts to LEO.
- As of 2018, NASA still doesn't have a working manned spacecraft capable of launch to LEO, let alone beyond.
- 2011 to 2018 is almost the same time frame it took NASA to design, build, test and launch 11 seemingly successful Apollo Moon missions.
- At present, there are only two countries capable of launching astronauts to LEO and that is China and Russia. None of these two countries has, as of yet, shown it has the technology to send manned missions beyond LEO.

- China had a space station, but recently, it fell out of LEO and its manned space program seems to be on hold.
- Russia still maintains its manned spacecraft launch capabilities to LEO with its Soyuz program.
- And since NASA doesn't have its own manned spacecraft capable of launch to LEO, it pays the Russian space agency to send its astronauts to the ISS.

Decades after the Apollo Moon missions, the reality is, NASA no longer has a working manned space program capable of launch to LEO. The only country capable of consistently launching astronauts to LEO is Russia, and that's with using 50-year-old technology.

Not exactly what one would call, *a thriving manned space program.*

Chapter 6 - Endnotes

[1] Michael D. Bjorkman, Eric L. Christiansen, Apollo and America's Moon landing program Apollo Meteoroid Shielding Design and Analysis at the Manned Spacecraft Center, pp. 14-15.

[2] Ibid., p. 25.

[3] IBTimes Website, September 21 2016 and YouTube video 'NASA Astronaut Don Pettit We Can't Go Back To The Moon.'

[4] Dwanye A. Day, Thunder in a bottle: the non-use of the mighty F-1 Engine, published March 27, 2006 on www.thespacereview.com

[5] NASA, The Apollo 11 Telemetry Data Recordings: A Final Report – Online Article, www.nasa.gov

[6] Ibid.

[7] Ibid.

[8] Ibid.

[9] Ibid.

[10] Ibid.

Glossary

AGC	Apollo Guidance Computer
AGS	Lunar Module's Abort Guidance System
ARS	Atmosphere Revitalization System
ASPO	Apollo Spacecraft Project Officer
BPC	Boost Protective Cover
CM	Command Module
CMEs	Coronal Mass Ejections
CMP	Command Module Pilot
CNP	Calculated Neutral Point
DSKY	Display and Keyboard
EVA	Extravehicular Activity
GCRs	Galactic Cosmic Rays
GN&C	Guidance Navigation and Control System
ISS	International Space Station
KSC	Kennedy Space Center
LEO	Low Earth Orbit
LES	Launch Escape System
LOI	Lunar Orbit Insertion
LOR	Lunar Orbit Rendezvous
MSC	Manned Spacecraft Center
MSFC	Marshall Space Flight Center
NAA	North American Aviation
PGNS	Primary Guidance and Navigation System
PTC	Passive Thermal Control
RCS	Reaction Control System
SAA	South Atlantic Anomaly
SCS	Stabilization and Control System
SLA	Spacecraft Lunar Module Adaptor
SM	Service Module

SPE	Solar Particle Event
SPS	Service Propulsion System
TCS	Thermal Control System
TEI	Trans Earth Insertion
TLI	Translunar Insertion

Bibliography

Allday, Jonathan	APOLLO IN PERSPECTIVE SPACEFLIGHT THEN AND NOW. IOP Publishing, Ltd., 2000
Attivissimo, Paolo	MOON HOAX: DEBUNKED! Finally, a no-nonsense, fact-filled rebuttal of "moon hoax" claims, for doubters and enthusiasts alike. Lulu.com publishing, 2013
Baker, David	NASA MISSION APOLLO 13 AS-508 APOLLO 13 1970 (including Saturn, CM-109, SM-109, LM-7) Owners' Workshop Manual An engineering insight into how NASA saved the crew of the failed moon mission. Zenith Press, 2013
Bassett, Peter	The Great Moon Landing Hoax, or was it?. CreateSpace Independent Publishing, 1st edition, 2015
Bennett, Mary and Percy, David S.	DARK MOON APOLLO AND THE WHISTLE-BLOWERS. Adventures Unlimited Press, 2001
Bennett, Mary DM	Orion, the Van Allen Belts & Space Radiation Challenges. Article published online, www.aulis.com, 2015
Biddle, Wayne	A Field Guide to RADIATION. Penguin Books, 2012
Birur, C. Gajanana	Spacecraft Thermal Control. BiblioGov, 2013

Bjorkman, Michael D.,	APOLLO and America's Moon Landing Program Apollo Meteoroid Shielding Design and Analysis at the Manned Spacecraft Center. Progressive Management Publications, 2013
Chaikin, Andrew	A MAN ON THE MOON THE VOYAGES OF THE APOLLO ASTRONAUTS. Penguin Books, 2007
English, Robert A., Benson Richard E., Bailey, J. Vernon, and Barnes, Charles M.	APOLLO EXPERIENCE REPORT-PROTECTION AGAINST RADIATION, NASA TN D-7080. March 1973
Harland, David M.	THE FIRST MEN ON THE MOON The Story of Apollo 11. Praxis Publishing, 2007
Ivchenkov, Gennady	Evaluation of F-1 characteristics, based on the analysis of heat transfer and strength of the tubular cooling jacket. Article published online, www.aulis.com, 2013
Kaysing, Bill	We Never Went To The Moon. Mokelumne Hill Publishing, 1976
Kranz, Gene	FAILURE IS NOT AN OPTION MISSION CONTROL FROM MERCURY TO APOLLO 13 AND BEYOND. Simon & Shuster, 2009
Lheureux, Philippe	Moon Landings: Did NASA Lie?. Carnot USA Books, 2003
Meseguer, J., Grande, Perez, Sanz-Andres, A.	Spacecraft thermal control. Woodhead Publishing Limited, 2012
Mindell, David A.	Digital Apollo Human and Machine in Spaceflight. MIT Press, 2011
Moldwin, Mark	AN INTRODUCTION TO SPACE WEATHER. Cambridge University Press, 2008

National Aeronautics And Space Administration	PROJECT APOLLO 11 LUNAR LANDING MISSION, PRESS KIT. Books Express Publishing, 2012
National Aeronautics And Space Administration, Manned Spacecraft Center	APOLLO SPACECRAFT NEWS REFERENCE. Apogee Prime, 2011
National Research Council Of The National Academies	Space Radiation Hazards and the Vision for Space Exploration. The National Academies Press, 2006
National Research Council Of the National Academies	Managing Space Radiation Risk in the New Era of Space Exploration. The National Academies Press, 2008
O'Brien, Frank	THE APOLLO GUIDANCE COMPUTER Architecture and Operation. Praxis Publishing, 2010
Pascal, Xavier	Was the Apollo Computer flawed? An investigation into Apollo computer documentation. Article published online, www.aulis.com, 2013
Pavlosky, James E., St. Leger, Leslie G.	APOLLO EXPERIENCE REPORT- THERMAL PROTECTION SUBSYSTEM, NASA TN D-7564. January 1974
Pokrovsky, S. G.	Investigation into the Saturn V velocity and its ability to place the stated payload into lunar orbit. Article published online, www.aulis.com, 2011
Pokrovsky, S. G.	Improved estimates of the Saturn V velocity and its ability to place the stated payload into lunar orbit. Article published online, www.aulis.com, 2011

Poppe, Barbara B., Jorden, Kristen P.	Sentinels of the Sun Forecasting Space Weather. Johnson Books, 2006
Reichl, Eugen	AMERICA IN SPACE SERIES PROJECT APOLLO THE EARLY YEARS, 1960-1967. Schiffer Publishing, Ltd, 2016
Reichl, Eugen	AMERICA IN SPACE SERIES PROJECT APOLLO THE MOON LANDINGS, 1968-1972. Schiffer Publishing, Ltd., 2017
Reichl, Eugen	AMERICA IN SPACE SERIES SATURN V AMERICA'S ROCKET TO THE MOON. Schiffer Publishing, Ltd., 2018
Rene, Ralph	NASA MOONED AMERICA! Originally published by R. Rene, 1992. This edition published by Jarrah White, 2011
Riley, Christopher and Dolling, Phil	NASA MISSION APOLLO 11 1969 (including Saturn V, CM-107, SM-107, LM-5) Owners' Workshop Manual And insight into the hardware from the first manned mission to land on the Moon. Haynes Publishing, 2015
Space Studies Board, Board On Atmospheric Sciences and Climate, National Research Council	Radiation And The International Space Station, Recommendations to Reduce Ricks. National Academy Press, 2000
Sprankle, Michael	I want to Believe. Independently published, 2017
Stakem, Patrick H.	Apollo's Computers. USA, PRRB Publishing, 2013
Stakem, Patrick H.	The Saturn V and the Pegasus Missions, 1965. PRRB Publishing, 2012
Walt, Martin	Introduction to Geomagnetically Trapped Radiation. Cambridge University Press, 2005

Woods, W. David	HOW APOLLO FLEW TO THE MOON. Praxis Publishing, 2010
Young, Anthony	The SATURN V F-1 ENGINE Powering Apollo into History. Praxis Publishing, 2009

Printed in Great Britain
by Amazon